MW00577343

The Ritual of
New Creation

SUNY Series in
Modern Jewish Literature and Culture

Sarah Blacher Cohen, Editor

The Ritual of
New Creation

Jewish Tradition and
Contemporary Literature

NORMAN FINKELSTEIN

STATE UNIVERSITY OF NEW YORK PRESS

Published by
State University of New York Press, Albany

© 1992   State University of New York

All rights reserved

Printed in the United States of America

No part of this book may be used or reproduced
in any manner whatsoever without written permission
except in the case of brief quotations embodied in
critical articles and reviews.

For information, address State University of New York
Press, State University Plaza, Albany, N.Y. 12246

Production by Ruth Fisher
Marketing by Dana E. Yanulavich

Library of Congress Cataloging-in-Publication Data

Finkelstein, Norman, 1954–
      The Ritual of New Creation : Jewish tradition and contemporary
    literature / Norman Finkelstein.
          p.   cm. — (SUNY series in modern Jewish literature and
    culture)
      Includes index.
      ISBN 0–7914–1089–7 (CH : acid-free) ISBN 0–7914–1090–0 (pbk.:
    acid-free)
      1. Jews—Intellectual life. 2. Judaism—20th century. 3. Bloom,
    Harold. 4. Scholem, Gershom Gerhard, 1897–   . 5. Ozick, Cynthia—
    Criticism and interpretation. 6. American literature—Jewish
    authors—History and criticism. I. Title. II. Series.
      DS113.F48   1992
      296.3'875—dc20
                                                          91–27776
                                                             CIP

10 9 8 7 6 5 4 3 2 1

Only radically atheistic ages
can thoroughly understand
what constitutes not the privilege
but the originality of Jewish culture.
If only they do not miss its poetry!

—OLIVIER REVAULT D'ALLONNES

for Ann and Steven

Contents

Contents

ACKNOWLEDGMENTS

I would like to thank the Faculty Development Committee and the Office of the Dean of Arts and Sciences of Xavier University for giving me a faculty development grant and reduced teaching loads during the years 1987–1990, during which time *The Ritual of New Creation* was conceived and written. To Sarah Blacher Cohen, the editor of the Modern Jewish Literature and Culture series at SUNY Press, my deep appreciation for her ongoing interest in my work. A number of sections of the book originally appeared in periodicals, sometimes in earlier versions. Chapter 2 was published in *Critical Texts* as "The Sage of New Haven." Chapter 4 appeared in *LIT: Literature, Interpretation, Theory,* under the title "The Struggle for Historicity in the Fiction of Cynthia Ozick." Part of Chapter 5 appeared in *Pequod* as "The Book In Tatters." My thanks to the editors of these periodicals. Part of Chapter 1 was presented at a symposium held at Baltimore Hebrew University on "The Culture of Jewish Modernity and the Post-Modern Turn"; I am grateful to Professor Alan Udoff for the invitation to speak at the symposium.

During the summer of 1990, while this book was nearing completion, I participated in the NEH summer seminar on Jewish-American literature at the University of Illinois-Chicago, directed by Professor Mark Krupnick. This experience provided me with the inspiration and ideas I needed to bring *The Ritual of New Creation* to its conclusion—many thanks to Professor Krupnick and my fellow participants.

Two cherished friends of long standing, one nearby and one far away, read, discussed, and often argued various parts of this book with me at length. On this occasion I extend my greetings and thanks to Ross Feld and Henry Weinfield. And finally, I am indebted to my wife Kathryn for her love and her support. I think she understands my relation to Jewish culture better than anyone else, myself included.

I gratefully acknowledge the following for having given me permission to quote from published work:

David R. Godine, Publisher, for permission to quote from *Chelmaxioms,* by Allen Mandelbaum, copyright 1977 by Allen Mandelbaum.

John Hollander, for permission to quote from *Spectral Emanations,* copyright 1978 by John Hollander.

Alfred A. Knopf, Inc., for permission to quote from *Harp Lake* by John Hollander, copyright 1988 by John Hollander; and from *The Collected Poems of Wallace Stevens* by Wallace Stevens, copyright 1954 by Wallace Stevens.

Persea Books Inc., for permission to quote from *The Poems of Paul Celan,* translated by Michael Hamburger, copyright 1988 by Michael Hamburger.

INTRODUCTION

This book has grown slowly. Even before it was really born, these words were spoken over it: "We no longer know just what makes a book Jewish, or a person Jewish, because we have no authority to instruct us as to what is or is not Jewish thought."[1] I felt my Jewishness deeply, but in what ways did it manifest itself? My daily life was lived on a completely secular plane, although I remained attracted to the old customs and rituals as to a remote but still beautiful poem. Raised as a Conservative Jew, I had ceased to believe in God long before, yet I was a rather pious atheist and brooded over the space He had vacated. Harold Bloom's bold assertion challenged me to ask questions of thought and culture which I had previously put aside.

The paths down which I pursued my answers had already been set before me by cultural heritage, personal temperament, and professional training. They were textual paths, and they confirmed for me, as Bloom elsewhere argues, that it is "text-centeredness" rather than any "religious idea" which distinguishes the modern Jewish sensibility.[2] While this notion, stated so bluntly, probably would be considered unacceptable (or at least inadequate) by most of those who seek for an understanding of Jewish identity, it has helped me nevertheless to imagine the role I wished to play as a reader, a critic, a commentator, as I began to focus on recent Jewish writing. For it is only in these capacities that I could situate myself at all in modern Jewish, and specifically modern Jewish-American life.

In an essay to which I return again and again, Gershom Scholem speaks of the development of rabbinic Judaism: "Not system but *commentary* is the legitimate form through which truth is approached."[3] It is this faith in commentary which survives, however translated, the entrance of Judaism onto the modern world-stage. However remote modern Jewish intellectuals seem to grow from traditional concerns, and no matter how directly and violently history may impose itself upon them, their projects and pursuits are peculiarly mediated by the book. "In the book, the Jew himself becomes a

1

book. In the Jew, the book itself becomes Jewish words. Because for
him, the book is more than confirmation, it is the revelation of his
Judaism."[4] In these lines, Edmond Jabès, typically, does not specify
the book he means. By now, the "secular" Jewish writer—a Bloom, a
Jabès—thinks less of Scripture than of the processes through which
Scripture has been disseminated. Regardless of what normative
Judaism still has to offer, Walter Benjamin's commentary on Kafka
remains paradigmatic for all Jewish intellectuals who cannot accept
the old ways:

> The gate to justice is learning. And yet Kafka does not dare
> attach to this learning the promises which tradition has
> attached to the study of the Torah. His assistants are sextons
> who have lost their house of prayer, his students are pupils
> who have lost the Holy Writ. Now there is nothing to sup-
> port them on their "untrammeled, happy journey."[5]

And so (to momentarily conflate Jabès and Benjamin), "the Jew
bends over his book" and goes, however ironically, on his "untrammeled, happy journey." This book is the record of one such journey.

So in writing this book I returned to certain authors, certain
texts, certain motifs again and again, and my readers surely will note
such obsessive, such ecstatic repetitions. All commentary, as I have
come to understand it, requires repetition; it produces Kierkegaard's
"remembering forward" or Bloom's "misreading" through which
commentators can, in the full paradox of the word, say something
original. My title will serve as an example. Readers familiar with
Scholem (one of those figures with whom I am most obsessed) will
recognize in it the key terms from the title of his "Tradition and New
Creation in the Ritual of the Kabbalists." In this essay, Scholem
demonstrates how the Kabbalists subtly reworked the rituals of
remembrance and sanctification which they found in rabbinic Judaism
into transformative, magical rituals. "The existing ritual was not
changed," Scholem tells us. "It was taken over more or less intact."[6]
The Kabbalists, given their passionate mythical intentions, followed
out the sober, inherited rituals, but changed them from within. The
result was a new creation that still accorded itself with the old ways.

The historical dialectics of religious thought and cultural attitude are subtle and full of irony: as Scholem argues, the messianic
crisis of kabbalism, culminating in the Sabbatian debacle, may well
have moved Judaism closer to the Haskalah and to its great receptivi-

ty to the forces of modernity. In modern times, ritual and the investment of faith which stood behind it have been cast radically into doubt. If ritual remains, it is preserved in the act of new creation itself. Contemporary Jewish writers, dwelling all their lives in a secular world but never quite at home (since when have Jews felt at home?), know only that in their books they perform this ritual of new creation. They honor the past *through* rupture because, as Yosef Hayim Yerushalmi tells us, their past has been a tradition *of* rupture.[7] Commentary, which becomes virtually synonymous with "Jewish writing," both records and enacts these longstanding conditions.

The themes which recur and overlap throughout this book are all related to what I have come to call the "modern ritual of new creation." To the extent that they are identifiable as distinct entities, I can name three: (1) the matter of secular literary activity; (2) the matter of "wandering meaning"; (3) the matter of loss and exile. These issues tend to resist narratization. Although they can be associated with the various writers whom I address directly (such as Bloom, Steiner, or Benjamin) or to whom I sometimes refer (such as Yerushalmi, Revault D'Allonnes, or Derrida), they most often appear at the borders of my discussions, insistently drawing my attention from specific authors and texts to larger cultural concerns. They constitute the essential subject matter of a work which is, paradoxically, deeply vexed by the very notion that there are essences in writing at all.

The first of my themes completely pervades the book and concerns every writer under discussion herein. The more I read modern Jewish authors, the more dubious I find the conventional polarity of religious and secular writing. Kafka was probably the first such author to fully articulate the problem, as in his famous diary entry concerning writing as an "assault on the last earthly frontier" which "might easily have developed into a new secret doctrine, a Kabbalah."[8] Bloom, meditating on this passage and its probable influence on Scholem, concludes by predicting that Kafka will become "the severest and most harassing of the belated sages of what will yet become the Jewish cultural tradition of the future."[9] Such a conflation of terms and traditions ("severest and most harassing" is taken from Wallace Stevens) underscores Bloom's declaration that "What I find incoherent is the judgment that some authentic literary art is more sacred or more secular than some other."[10] The literary imagination escapes or resists these supposedly antithetical categories, or as a deconstructionist would say, collapses this binary opposition.

It is just through these troubled oppositions and resistances that "the Jewish cultural tradition of the future" is being born. Even writers with what appear to be more normative orientations cannot avoid this issue. George Steiner, for example, insists that meaning is dependent upon "a wager on transcendence" which he believes to stand behind the production and reception of all works of art.[11] By calling in "our debts to theology and the metaphysics of presence,"[12] Steiner challenges us to reconsider just what occurs when we enter the ineluctably ritualistic sphere of creativity. The need for this reconsideration is especially pertinent for Jewish textuality: the traditional Jewish emphasis on writing, which survives (and participates in) the crisis of modernity, continually reminds us of the *contractual* relationship of the Jews to God, even when that contract appears to be void.[13] Jewish writing, to move from Steiner's terms to those of Cynthia Ozick, "touches on the liturgical." For like Steiner (although she argues with him), Ozick insists that a religious sensibility is always at work in significant literary production. Indeed, Ozick goes so far as to say that "The secular Jew is a figment; when a Jew becomes a secular person he is no longer a Jew. This is especially true for makers of literature."[14] This statement is valuable because it is blunt and to the point, but in regard to literature at least, it merely returns us to our original problem: how can we describe that quality we call "Jewish" which we find in a Jewish writer?[15] If it is not a matter of a specific religious propensity (and I, for one, do not believe it is, since I maintain the validity of the notion of the secular Jew), then what aspects of Jewish writing must we investigate?

This leads me to my second theme, that of "wandering meaning," a term which I borrow once more from Bloom, specifically from his discussion of Revault d'Allonnes and Freud. Seeing in the Freudian transference "a synecdoche for all the Jewish metamorphoses of exile into achievement," Bloom then makes an important generalization: "The wandering people has taught itself and others the lesson of wandering meaning, a wandering that has compelled a multitude of changes in the modes of interpretation available to the West."[16] I am deeply impressed by the endurance and applicability of this notion, which once again strikes me as the kind of idea that is more pertinent to modern Jewish writing than any normative belief. Wandering and transformation imply process, movement, change of state. But how far can Jewish writing wander, to what extent can it be transformed, before we say it has gone too far, it has changed too much?

A range of answers emerges. At one extreme we find an author like Jabès with his notorious conflation of writing and Judaism as "*one and the same waiting, one and the same hope, one and the same wearing down.*"[17] Jabès believes that (at least for himself) the process of writing is completely congruent with the process of discovering Jewish self-identity. And because he defines modernity as openness, which he names in turn the basic condition of the book, Jewish identity remains open and individualized.[18] Jabès's chain of metonyms—modernity-openness-the book-the writer-the Jew—enacts the processes of wandering and transformation. In one of his essays on Jabès, Derrida links such writing to one of the central insights of deconstruction:

> Just as there is a negative theology, there is a negative atheology. An accomplice of the former, it still pronounces the absence of a center, when it is play that should be affirmed. But is not the desire for a center, as a function of play itself, the indestructible itself? And in the repetition or return of play, how could the phantom of the center not call to us? It is here that the hesitation between writing as decentering and writing as an affirmation of play is infinite.[19]

For Derrida and Jabès, modern Jewish writing in particular is constituted by this infinite hesitation between negative atheology and the affirmation of play.

The extremity of this stance is tempered in Bloom's project, in which, as we have seen, text-centeredness is the sine qua non of Jewish writing and identity. But for Bloom, the presence of a literary tradition stabilizes writing: in their agonistic relationship to their precursors, strong writers are both individualized and situated in an ongoing textual community, however strained relations may be within such a group. Meaning wanders, to be sure, but only insofar as there are texts through which it can wander. Jewish identity and Jewish writing are less metonyms for this dynamic than they are indispensable examples. It is difficult to ascertain, finally, if Bloom's theory of writing is drawn from Judaism or projected onto it, but then, it is just such distinctions that Bloom's work criticizes.

We can say, however, that Bloom occupies something of a middle ground in the debate over wandering Jewish meaning. He is situated closely to his precursors, Scholem and Benjamin. When Benjamin speaks of the changing relation of aggadah to halakah in his interpretation of Kafka, or when Scholem discusses the strange combination of awe and presumptuousness in the relation of commentator to scripture, we encounter fluid but nonetheless definable textual categories. These categories, however much they undergo change, have operated continually in the domain of Jewish writing, which is not, then, merely congruent with the indeterminacy of writing itself.

But there are those who would stabilize the notion of Jewish writing to an even greater extent. The contemporary tendency to conflate literary theory and traditional Jewish textuality has led to an extraordinary debate, which is, fortunately, shedding as much light as heat on what could be called the identity crisis of Jewish writing. Against what they regard as the extravagance of post-structuralist claims on Jewish writing, cautious and responsible scholars have sought to delineate Jewish textual traditions from more recent developments, while at the same time acknowledging parallels and even influences.[20] These scholars (who might well cast a cold eye on some passages in this book) have provided an important service by carefully explaining many of the intricacies of aggadah, midrash, and kabbalah: indeed, we are witnessing a renaissance of traditional Jewish studies, but one which must also take literary theory into account. As David Stern observes, "The difference separating these conceptions is at least one sign of the distance that interpretation has traveled in the course of history."[21]

So meaning has wandered and continues to wander; whether one is an advocate of writerly freeplay or scholarly definitiveness, the trope itself seems unavoidable in any discussion of Jewish literature. The reason for this, of course, is that for Jews, wandering is far more than a trope: it is a historical given. If, in what I have said up until now, history tends to appear as a fold in the text, then in the matter of exile, the text must appear as a fold in history. Loss and exile, the third of my themes, however much they lend themselves to literary matters, insistently point to the unstable boundary between the book and the world. "Our Homeland, the Text": here we are reminded of the enduring historical substitution of textual rootlessness for geopolitical ground, which, in George Steiner's crucial formulation, achieves its most probing, most disturbing modern articulation.

I do not think we can speak of the Jewish experience of exile and the concomitant Jewish devotion to the text, even when they are coupled with utopian and messianic longings for restoration, as constituting a single ideology. Aside from the term's connotation of "false consciousness" which the presence of the utopian and the messianic serve to mitigate,[22] belief-systems, and more importantly, practices of writing derived from the conditions of diaspora vary greatly, in keeping with the extraordinary diversity of modern Jewish thought. Writing in itself may be the ne plus ultra of diasporic culture, but the role which exile plays in writing still must be determined, for the most part, in terms of the individual author and the individual work. If we can speak of loss as being inscribed, then each Jewish author inscribes the experience of exile through his or her unique economy of writing.

Having claimed this, I must also admit that in another sense, exile is always already inscribed upon Jewish writers' texts. In his great essay on the Messianic idea, Gershom Scholem describes this sense:

> The magnitude of the Messianic idea corresponds to the endless powerlessness in Jewish history during all the centuries of exile, when it was unprepared to come forward onto the plane of world history. There's something preliminary, something provisional about Jewish history; hence its inability to give of itself entirely. For the Messianic idea is not only consolation and hope. Every attempt to realize it tears open the abysses which lead each of its manifestations *ad absurdum*. There is something grand about living in hope, but at the same time there is something profoundly unreal about it. It diminishes the singular worth of the individual, and he can never fulfill himself, because the incompleteness of his endeavors eliminates precisely what constitutes its highest value. Thus in Judaism the Messianic idea has compelled a *life lived in deferment,* in which nothing can be done definitively, nothing can be irrevocably accomplished.[23]

The condition adumbrated by Scholem in this passage is of particular moment for modern Jewish writers. If the overdetermined force of exile produces, through the Messianic idea, a radical incompleteness in Jewish life, then Jewish writers are faced with continual frustration. Unable to effect what might be called an existential closure in their work, they are compelled to accept *the exile of the text,* living, as Derrida says, "the necessity of interpretation as an exile."[24] But if Scholem is correct, it is this very exile which, however much it diminishes personal achievement, maintains the work of hope.

It may seem difficult to imagine the authoritative utterances of a Bloom or a Steiner as provisional; even the high comedy of Cynthia

Ozick's stories or Allen Mandelbaum's poetry, however infused with exilic longing, strikes us as notably assertive and definitive. Yet we are still dealing here with writers, however magisterial they may sound, who deeply intuit that, as Mandelbaum says,

> Diaspora
> is still the way
> of shreds and shards,
> of all that frays,
> discolored words,
> and leaves astray,
> and winds that scatter
> nesting birds...[25]

Perhaps this is what Benjamin understood when he spoke of even Kafka's work as having "the purity and beauty of a failure."[26] Few Jewish writers have done so well in failing, for it was a failure which, in its lack, most fully expressed the messianic condition of exile. Small comfort though it may be for Kafka's literary descendents, failure remains a badge of honor for writing in, for writing as, exile.

Having defined the pervasive themes of this study, it remains for me to describe the progress of its chapters, which can be understood conceptually and, to some extent, stylistically as well. Along with this Introduction, my first chapter, on Postmodernism and the Jewish literary intellectual, is the most generalizing section of the book; it is to be read as a meditation on some of the contemporary forces affecting Jewish writing, as well as the place of that writing in the culture at large. Some of the issues raised in this chapter, notably those which concern the problematic of Jewish tradition, are then developed in chapters dealing with Harold Bloom and Gershom Scholem, two figures who, from their original areas of expertise, have gone on to have great influence on the way we understand the overall workings of modern Jewish thought and writing.

Growing increasingly specific, I next examine some representative literary texts. In the work of Cynthia Ozick, John Hollander and Allen Mandelbaum, we see the ways in which the cultural and literary themes identified in the earlier part of the book are worked through in relation to the specific generic demands of prose fiction and of poetry. This line of inquiry culminates in a chapter on George Steiner, one of the few Jewish literary intellectuals today who can still lay claim to that old-fashioned, even troubling, but still powerful title of "man of letters." As a theorist, a practical critic, and a novelist, Steiner compells me to broaden my perspective again, as does his doubly authoritative rhetoric of cosmopolitan, universalizing culture and of specifically Jewish tradition.

The Ritual of New Creation ends in a different but certainly related key, with two "writerly" chapters, one focused on an individual, one on a mood. My consideration of Walter Benjamin self-consciously appropriates a frequently observed but rarely engaged aspect of his work: his creation of fragmented "constellations" of ideas resulting in a "dialectic at a standstill," a means of writing which I consider to be particularly appropriate for a discussion of his messianic thought. My final chapter, on nostalgia and futurity in contemporary Jewish culture, is meant to complement the meditation on Postmodernism in Chapter 1. These last sections, more than any that precede them, are meant to be read as enactments of the Jewish ritual of new creation I have discussed above. Their relation to the tradition of Jewish writing is midrashic, which is to say that in ritually troping on the past, they intend to create a space for themselves in whatever comes to be understood as the Jewish cultural tradition of the future.

▲

CHAPTER 1

Postmodernism and the Jewish Literary Intellectual

Though the two terms which constitute the title of this chapter are both rather amorphous, they have decidedly different and variously revealing histories. Secular by definition, culturally heterogeneous, and inspired by the urgent need to rescue the past, Jewish literary intellectuals always come to us bearing a specific historical pedigree. More often than not, they are examples of Isaac Deutscher's "non-Jewish Jew," who have "found Jewry too narrow, too archaic, and too constricting."[1] Yet they bear the mark of their Jewish heritage in that they live "on the borderlines of nations and religions" and can "comprehend more clearly the great movement and the great contra-dictoriness of nature and society."[2] This dialectical understanding extends to the contradictions of secular literature, to which modern Jewish intellectuals nevertheless cling as do traditional Jews to the Law. We must think of such figures in the way that Yosef Hayim Yerushalmi insists that the modern Jewish historian think about him-self: as "a product of rupture." For Yerushalmi, Jewish history itself entails "ruptures, breaches, breaks," a series of losses and salvage operations which modern Jews deny only at great social and spiritual risk. No wonder that Walter Benjamin has become the paradigmatic Jewish literary intellectual of our century. The particular fate of such a man and his work in what had become the maw of Western Civi-lization appears to us now with, to use his own expression, an auratic intensity that seems to be the light of historicity itself.

If the notion of the Jewish literary intellectual invites histori-cization, then Postmodernism in the arts and human sciences resists such treatment. Recent fiery discussions of Postmodernism are certainly worth considering, but can they be said to constitute its history? Given Postmodernism's antipathy to historical understanding, the very notion of its history would be laughable if it were not so important to our current state of affairs. Postmodernism involves a strong suspicion, if not outright rejection of the frame of historical knowledge; nevertheless, there are occasions when we must impose such a frame, treating Postmodernism with unwonted critical rigor. As Fredric Jameson observes of the Postmodern's disturbingly playful treatment of history, "the resurrection of the dead of anonymous and silenced generations, the retrospective dimension indispensable to any vital reorientation of our collective future—has meanwhile itself become a vast collection of images, a multitudinous photographic simulacrum."[3] Confronted by this Postmodern simulacrum, it becomes increasingly difficult to engage in that project, both Marxist and Jewish, set forth by Benjamin in a sentence that no doubt Jameson is recalling: "Only that historian will have the gift of fanning the spark of hope in the past who is firmly convinced that *even the dead* will not be safe from the enemy if he wins."[4]

The questions I must pose, then, are difficult ones, in that their terms are so variously intractable. What happens to Jewish literary intellectuals, imbued as they are with both a strong historical perspective and with the morality of that perspective, when they encounter a cultural tendency which has as one of its most salient qualities the insistent leveling of historical heights and depths? How do thinkers who inhabit a world of voices echoing over long distances respond to a startlingly immediate environment of sheer surface and explosive multiplication of images? What attraction would Postmodernism, with its cool exploitation of perpetual rupture, its paradoxical shaping of brilliant, superficial changes into what Benjamin calls "*Das Immergleich*," the ever-the-same, have for those who brood continually over breaks and restorations in a historical continuum that is all too palpably real? In short, how can we continue to ponder civilization and its discontents when David Byrne urges us to "stop making sense"?

At first glance, the answer to these questions appears relatively straightforward: Jewish writers and critics, both in the United States and abroad, tend to resist the blandishments of Postmodernism. Cynthia Ozick's critique of Postmodern fiction as idolatrous comes to mind, as does Marshall Berman's strong distinction between Modernism and Postmodernism, with his insistence on the continued viability of the former and the static nihilism of the latter.[5] In France, which can be considered the home ground of theoretical Postmodernism, Olivier Revault d'Allonnes opposes the deconstruction of the human subject with what he calls "the duty of inwardness."[6] In a different register, Saul Friedlander identifies the "neutralization" of history and a kind of Postmodern kitsch in a number of important novels and films and associates them with the most insidious of all forms of kitsch, that of Nazism.[7] Indeed, the cultural promiscuity which Jameson labels "the nostalgia mode,"[8] so remote from Benjamin's revolutionary nostalgia, covers a great deal of the territory we have come to know as the Postmodern. Could such blithely threatening cultural amnesia maintain an attraction to Jewish intellectuals, steeped as they are in what Berman recognizes as a tradition of progressive modernity? Jean-Francois Lyotard defines the Postmodern "as incredulity toward metanarratives."[9] A long line of secular Jewish intellectuals took a great part in the original composition of those metanarratives: who among their contemporary heirs really would find them incredible?

If (according to Lyotard), Postmodernism represents an epistemological as well as a cultural transformation, and if (according to Jameson), Postmodernism is to be understood not as a mere style but as a full-blown "cultural dominant," then Jewish intellectuals' relative assimilation or rejection of the Postmodern is of great moment, and not only to Jewish traditions of thought and writing. I have said that at the outset, it would appear that the Jewish intellectual response is one of caution, suspicion, resistance and repudiation to a cultural tendency which displays an aggressive indifference to history. Jews were in the vanguard of Modernism because Modernism defined itself historically as a rupture, the inception of a permanent cultural revolution. This sense of historical agon was in turn intensified by Jewish contributions to Modernist production in the all the arts and sciences. The wild dialectic of Modernist exhilaration and despair, that sense of history accelerating to the breaking point which Berman describes so well in *All That Is Solid Melts Into Air*, takes on, for the Jews, a special poignancy, as the general crisis of modernization is compounded by the specific crisis of assimilation.

This particularly Jewish dialectical intensity—in a sophisticated but deeply torn figure such as Benjamin it amounts to a pathos—may also be at the heart of the apparently benign, general definition of the literary intellectual at which Berman's mentor, Lionel Trilling, arrives:

Less committed to method and to fact than the philosopher
or the social scientist, licensed in emotion and intuition by the
tradition of the subject he has studied, he ranges freely and
directs his arguments to man-in-general. It is he who shows
the most indignant face in moral and cultural dispute and who
is most apt to assume that the intellectual life is dramatic.[10]

This passage has just the hint of autobiography, and I will have more
to say about Trilling himself later. For now, I want to speculate that
Berman's understanding of Modernism's whirlwind progress or
Trilling's emphasis on the literary intellectual's sense of indignation
and drama in cultural dispute is at least informed by, if not altogether
the product of that secular Judaism which is coincidental with Modernism itself. The great flowering of secular Jewish intellectual life in
the nineteenth and early twentieth centuries enters into a crucial
dialectic, lives out a great drama with the general rise of Modernist
culture. As Jews entered the mainstream of Western cultural life,
Judaism was to be remade under the aegis of modernity. Kafka is one
of our best and most obvious examples: of his father's weakened,
transitional Judaism, Kafka says that "precisely the getting rid of it
seemed to me to be the devoutest action,"[11] but he still studies
Hebrew and Yiddish and, as I noted in my Introduction, longs for a
literature that "might easily have developed into a new secret doctrine, a Kabbalah."

But there is a price to be paid before the recently Westernized
Jew of culture produces his Modernist Kabbalah and presents it to
either a Jewish or a Gentile readership. I am referring to what John
Murray Cuddihy calls "the ordeal of civility." Contributing to Western culture, even when one's contribution is radically Modernistic,
cannot occur before one undergoes the process of "refinement." As
Cuddihy observes in his discussion of the Jewish aspects of psychoanalysis:

The "shock" of Jewish Emancipation had come first. Lured
by the promise of civil rights, Jews in the nineteenth century
were disillusioned to find themselves not in the *pays légale* of
a political society but in the *pays réel* of a civil society. Lured
by the promise of becoming *citoyens,* they found that they
had first to become *bourgeois.* The ticket of admission to
European society was not baptism, as Heine thought, but
Bildung and behavior.[12]

For the late nineteenth-century Jews of Vienna, Freud "was their self-appointed intellectual elite, mediating them over into the promises and perils of modernity."[13] The psychoanalytic method opened a private space in civil society, in which the neurotic Jewish patient could deal with the traumatic past, including the family past of unacceptable shtetl behavior. Freud's discoveries, of course, became a universalizing science because the psychological dilemma of Viennese Jewry was an acute example of a pervasive malaise, the personal price paid for modernity by Western society. Still, psychoanalysis remains the special purview of secular Jews, and it is no accident that Philip Roth, whose novels straddle the fence between Modernism and Postmodernism, writes his most notorious work as a parody of a tortured Jewish session on the couch. From Freud to Roth, Jewish Modernism couples exorbitant alienation with scrutinizing critical intellect. The result is usually an affront to refined sensibilities.

Here we have another reason for the Jewish literary intellectual's probable difficulty with Postmodernism. Jameson states that between Modernism and Postmodernism, there is a "shift in the dynamics of cultural pathology [which] can be characterized as one in which the alienation of the subject is displaced by the fragmentation of the subject."[14] On the theoretical level, this correlates to post-structuralism's critique of the centered human subject. Likewise, Postmodern works of art "are now free-floating and impersonal, and tend to be dominated by a peculiar kind of euphoria," as in, say, the poems of John Ashbery or the fiction of Thomas Pynchon. But self-conscious Jewish writers and intellectuals, I would argue, tend to be wed to what Jameson calls "the older *anomie* of the centred subject":[15] not only do they cling, however nostalgically, to history and to cultural metanarratives, they cling to their selves too, however anxiety-ridden they might be.

Postmodernism's failure to seize the Jewish literary imagination does not mean, however, that Jewish intellectuals are not affected by the Postmodern environment in which they must inevitably operate. Indeed, if my extrapolation of Trilling's definition is at all correct and Jewish literary intellectuals are particularly prone to the disputatious drama of cultural life, then the controversy, the scandal of the Postmodern is bound to attract them.

Take, for example, the seductive power of that "multitudinous photographic simulacrum," the infinitely expanding image-world which Benjamin, with his usual prescience, called to our attention so long ago. Benjamin's ambivalence toward what would eventually grow into the totalizing sphere of the mass media is expressed in the counterpoint of his two great essays "The Storyteller" and "The Work of Art in the Age of Mechanical Reproduction," the former mourning the loss of auratic culture, the latter celebrating its destruction by the reproducible image. "The technique of reproduction detaches the reproduced object from the domain of tradition," notes Benjamin, and yet it is this "tremendous shattering of tradition which is the obverse of the contemporary crisis and renewal of mankind."[16] Benjamin's doubts about multiplying images are deeply Jewish, for such practices oppose the Second Commandment, a point which Cynthia Ozick never ceases to make in her excoriations of contemporary writing. Yet Benjamin is as much the secular Jewish intellectual in his messianic fascination with the twentieth-century technologies of the image, for a long and serious consideration of that which was traditionally deemed *assur*—forbidden—strongly marks Jewish intellectual life since the Haskalah.

But Postmodernism does not only fuel the drama of Jewish cultural thought through the provocation of ambivalent responses: at least one important Postmodern notion speaks directly to Jewish intellectuals' self-conception, their understanding of their obviously vexed Jewish identity and the role they play in the greater drama of culture at large. Consider the following portentous statement:

> First consequence: *différance* is not. It is not a present being, however excellent, unique, principal, or transcendent. It governs nothing, reigns over nothing, and nowhere exercises any authority. It is not announced by any capital letter. Not only is there no kingdom of *différance*, but *différance* instigates the subversion of every kingdom. Which makes it obviously threatening and infallibly dreaded by everything within us that desires a kingdom, the past or future presence of a kingdom. And it is always in the name of a kingdom that one may reproach *différance* with wishing to reign, believing that one sees it aggrandize itself with a capital letter.[17]

As articulated in one of Derrida's seminal post-structuralist essays, *différance*, which the philosopher expressly forbids us from understanding as a positive philosophical or "ontotheological" concept, certainly must be implicated in the Postmodern self-understanding of Jewish literary intellectuals. Derrida's work and his very figure as a product of secular Jewish culture constitute a border between the modern Jew of culture and the Postmodern Jew of *différance*. On an intellectual if not a psychosocial plane, *différance* means an end to the ordeal of civility and a palpable Jewish return of the repressed.

Différance produces itself through the production of differences. Thus if modernity rends the individual from the social fabric, Postmodernity as *différance* subverts both the individual and the social fabric in their entireties. And as Derrida says, "If the word 'history' did not in and of itself convey the motif of a final repression of difference, one could say that only differences can be 'historical' from the outset and in each of their aspects."[18] For Jewish writers and critics, this situation is of special moment. Through the assertion of difference, Jewish intellectuals reveal their historical—or better, their counterhistorical—aspect. Secular, largely assimilated, they speak of culture and to culture, knowing all the while that culture itself can be understood as a play of differences. Yet they do not dissolve completely into this play of differences, the nihilistic void on the edge of which thinkers like Derrida always tread. They cleave to the narratives of culture, including that of Judaism itself—a narrative of difference from which they are free to speak.

Put quite simply, Jewish intellectuals operating under the nonconcept, the negative force of *différance,* are more aggressively Jewish than their earlier modern counterparts, who labored under an ameliorating vision of humanism, usually aligned to a liberal or leftist political agenda. As Mark Shechner explains,

> It is not mistaken to regard Marxism, at a certain moment of its penetration into Jewish existence, as a substitute Judaism, endowed with all the powers once possessed by halakhic or Orthodox Judaism for interpreting the world, dictating principles, forming character, and regulating conduct. When it collapsed for those intellectuals, the event was no less disorienting for them than the dissolution of traditional Jewish life under Halakha had been for their grandparents.[19]

The dissolution of what was once a relatively stable ideological foundation makes up the tale of that generation of Jewish intellectuals usually associated with the *Partisan Review.* This process of dissolution (for Shechner it consists primarily of a movement through socialism and psychoanalysis, "a series of apostasies, losses, and disillusionments") inadvertently discouraged the direct incorporation of identifiably Jewish modes of thought and of textuality into their

work. Ironically, it could well be that the present generation represents a return to a more definite Jewish identity, though it is one that
has surely gone through the crucible of modernism.

I do not mean to say that the earlier Jewish intellectuals failed
to identify and write about their Jewishness in a variety of ways. Yet
there is a great difference between books like Alfred Kazin's *New
York Jew* or Irving Howe's *World of Our Fathers* on the one hand,
and Cynthia Ozick's *Art and Ardor* or Geoffrey Hartman's *Criticism
in the Wilderness* on the other. Among writers of the earlier generation, Judaism (or perhaps I should say an individual's Jewish identity)
is to be understood from a socio-historical perspective: to be a Jew
means to have a certain origin, a certain relation to society, a certain
set of cultural goals. For the following generation, all of these conditions obtain, but in addition Judaism provides a relatively detailed
intellectual infrastructure and a creative, formative idea as well as a
unique social milieu.

In order to speak more definitely about this shift in what we can
call "the sociology of knowledge" pertaining to Jewish literary intellectuals, I would like to compare two critics, both extremely influential in their time: Lionel Trilling and Harold Bloom. Trilling, who
died in 1975 after a career of over forty years, appears to us across the
abyss opened by recent developments in literary theory as a figure
from the history of criticism. But as Mark Krupnick reminds us in his
excellent study of Trilling, "the fate of cultural criticism" of the kind
Trilling produced has been largely an unfortunate one, especially due
to the split between increasingly specialized academic writing and a
waning tradition of intellectual journalism.[20] Readers rarely grant the
same authority to critics today as they once did; and few literary intellectuals feel comfortable making the great moral generalizations
which Trilling was apparently licensed to offer. The drama of cultural
debate through which one could emerge as a critic-hero has given way
before a general skepticism of the critical will to power. And yet it is
just such a role—elder statesman if not cultural *nabi*—to which
Harold Bloom seems to aspire. For after years of defiantly recondite
theorizing, Bloom at sixty emerges in his recent *Ruin the Sacred
Truths*—his Charles Eliot Norton Lectures—as a centralizing voice,
"the Yiddisher Dr. Johnson."

Here, of course, is the difference. It is not merely that Jews are
now thoroughly at home in the American academy; it is also that
Jewish literary accomplishments in the mainstream of intellectual discourses of late have drawn self-consciously upon Jewish sources.

The story of Trilling and the Columbia English Department is well known: informed that "as a Freudian, a Marxist, and a Jew" he would be "more comfortable elsewhere,"[21] Trilling, according to Sidney Hook, was near despair. Certain that genteel anti-Semitism was the root cause of his failure to be retained, Trilling sought Hook's advice. Hook recalls urging his friend to confront the Chairman directly, accusing the Department of bigotry, an act that for the mild-mannered Trilling was completely out of character.[22] Whether or not Trilling really acted on this advice (Hook says he did; Diana Trilling has a different version of the events), he succeeded in getting rehired. Here we have a true case of the ordeal of civility, a legendary single instance of aggressively Jewish self-identification in a career otherwise noted for urbane assimilation. For Alfred Kazin, with his stronger ties to lower-class Jewry, Trilling

> seemed intent on not diminishing his career by a single word. At our very first meeting in *The New Republic,*...Trilling astonished me by saying, very firmly, that he would not write anything that did not "promote my reputation."...Although I found so much solemnity about one's reputation hilarious, I was impressed by the tight-lipped seriousness with which Trilling said "my reputation." It seemed to resemble an expensive picture on view. "My reputation" was to be nursed along like money in the bank. It was capital. I had never encountered a Jewish intellectual so conscious of social position, so full of adopted finery in his conversation.[23]

Granted, this is as much gossip as sociological analysis, and to balance the picture I should note that Diana Trilling says of her husband that "It was not his sense that life was a contest of minds or that intellect was a weapon; it was more an instrument of conscience."[24] But whether one is reading Hook, Kazin, or Diana Trilling, what emerges from the portraits of Lionel Trilling is that quality of refinement which Cuddihy directly links to both modernity and the problem of Jewish assimilation.

In Trilling's criticism, this quality is translated into his ubiquitous concern for what he called "manners and morals," a concern derived equally from Arnold and Freud—both of whom, of course, variously study the balance of Hebraism and Hellenism in modern Western culture. In "Manners, Morals, and the Novel" (1947), Trilling identifies manners as a culture's hum and buzz of implication. I mean the whole evanescent context in which its explicit statements are made. It is that part of a culture which is made up of half-uttered or unuttered or unutterable expressions of value. They are hinted at by small actions, sometimes by the arts of dress or decoration, sometimes by tone, gesture, emphasis, or rhythm, sometimes by the words that are used with a special frequency or a special meaning.... They make the part of culture which is not art, or religion, or morals, or politics, and yet it relates to all these highly formulated departments of culture.[25]

These fine nuances and gradations of social behavior as elaborately detailed in the texts about which Trilling wrote and lectured, defined his task as a literary critic, and they remained his primary concern when he frequently ventured beyond literature into the broader, more inclusive realm of cultural criticism. In Trilling's hands, the text becomes an occasion for moral discrimination both by author and reader. But while the text is thus saved from reductionistic formalism (remember the hegemony of the Anglo-Catholic New Criticism through much of Trilling's career), it remains oddly confined to matters of social propriety and individual worth. Trilling was never really a political critic as would be more rigorously understood by a Georg Lukács or a Terry Eagleton: his early departure from Marxism toward a self-critical form of liberalism marks his work as a long series of struggles between the modern conscience, informed as it is by the dark knowledge of the cultural super-ego, and the exigent stuff of modern history.

How clear this becomes in *Sincerity and Authenticity* (1972), a true work of the center, in which the blandishments of authentic personal experience are finally rejected in favor of the admittedly old-fashioned concept of the sincere self whose personal truth is achieved through a public role. It is no accident that authenticity is aligned in the book's last chapter to a seminal work of Postmodern theory, Foucault's *Madness and Civilization*. Against the profoundly misguided view "that madness is liberation and authenticity," "each one of us a Christ," the refined Trilling, without the slightest irony, celebrates the real Christ's richly social career "of undertaking to intercede, of being a sacrifice, of reasoning with rabbis, of making sermons, of have disciples, of going to weddings and to funerals."[26]

Such Christian usages are rare in Trilling, but then again, Jewish references in his criticism are equally rare. On one revealing and prescient occasion, however, he did write about a Jewish text at some length. In "Wordsworth and the Rabbis" (1950), Trilling draws a fascinating comparison between Wordsworth's attitude toward Nature and the rabbinic attitude toward Torah as seen in the *Pirke Aboth*. His intention is to demonstrate that what was then Wordsworth's unacceptability, his lack of popularity, his canonic devaluation, was due to certain peculiarly non-Western, "Judaic" qualities in his work. The essay hinges on the following points:

> All that I want to suggest is the community of ideal and sensibility between the *Aboth* and the canon of Wordsworth's work—the passionate contemplation and experience of the great object which is proximate to Deity; then the plain living that goes with the high thinking, the desire for the humble life and the discharge of duty; and last, but not least important, a certain insouciant acquiescence in the anomalies of the moral order of the universe, a respectful indifference to, or graceful surrender before, the mysteries of the moral relation of God to man.[27]

Against this life-affirming quietism of Wordsworth and the Rabbis, Trilling sets the more typically Western concept of spiritual prestige as "some form of aggressive action directed upon the world, or inward upon ourselves," a religious idea represented in modern literature by T. S. Eliot's emphasis on violent martyrdom.[28]

"Wordsworth and the Rabbis" represents the limit of Trilling's ordeal of civility and of his cultural relationship to Judaism. His choice of a Jewish text is especially significant: the *Pirke Aboth* is one of the classics of normative Judaism, and the religious and social vision which Trilling sees there and in Wordsworth can certainly be considered a pillar of Western manners and morals. Against Eliot's violent Christianity and the New Critical denigration of the Romantic ethos, Trilling makes an equal claim for the centrality of a Jewish moral vision to Western culture. But in doing so, he must draw upon a version of Judaism—the "normal mysticism" of the Talmud—which deemphasizes heroism, struggle, and what we have come to call "difference."[29] As Mark Shechner observes, Judaism (or "rabbinism") can be regarded as congruent with Trilling's centralizing "anglophilia":

> Trilling's anglophilia was wholly consistent with his rabbinism, its fulfillment rather than its contradiction, and he

> became more the Jew by becoming more the Victorian. The
> catalyst for this daring gambit was Matthew Arnold, Trilling's
> guide to the nineteenth century and his ideal Hebraist, his
> master in strictness of conscience.... Trilling's brand of
> anglophilia, one suspects, was a back door Judaism after all,
> with the novel its Torah and criticism its commentary.[30]

This "back door Judaism," when it identifies itself as Judaism at all, is
refined and civil, sincere in precisely the way Trilling came to use the
term later in his career. Thus, Judaism becomes available to Trilling's
criticism only when it contributes to the moral, centralizing drive of
the project; Judaism's *différance,* both founder *and* other for Western culture, is anxiously avoided.

By contrast, Judaism is a central constituent in the work of
Harold Bloom, and this centrality of Judaism (or perhaps I should
say Judaisms) has contributed in turn to what has been through
much of his career a fiercely oppositional stance. Bloom, whose
ambivalence toward Derrida's thought is matter of record, would no
doubt feel uneasy being regarded as the embodiment of contemporary Jewish *différance.* Besides, by now a number of the key terms in
Bloom's work have found their way into our critical lexicon, and his
allegiance to a long line of obviously canonical authors—despite his
unorthodox readings of them—certainly moves him toward cultural
centrality. At a number of points in his career, Bloom takes issue with
the notion of modernism itself, seeing it merely as a weak and
unconvincing form of revision, and his comments regarding Postmodernism are even more dismissive. Nevertheless, if Postmodern
thought has any real bearing on Jewish literary intellectuals, Bloom,
perhaps more than any other contemporary, merits our attention.

To be modern is to experience rupture; to be Postmodern is to
reflect upon the experience of rupture, and in doing so repeat and
further that experience. In such works as *Kabbalah and Criticism,*
Bloom demonstrates that the interpretive paradigms which obtain in
some of the most esoteric Jewish texts likewise obtain in the canon of
secular literature, and that those paradigms depend as much upon
agon and breakage as they do upon tradition and continuity. He
comes to believe, as in a recent formulation, in "the stubborn resistance of imaginative literature to the categories of sacred and secular.... Poetry and belief wander about, together and apart, in a cos-
mological emptiness marked by the limits of truth and meaning."[31] If,
as Bloom claims, Jewish modernity thus means Kafka and Freud, then

Jewish Postmodernity means Bloom himself, who speculates that Kafka and Freud, along with Gershom Scholem, may someday "be seen as having redefined Jewish culture among them."[32] From seeing the religious past in the secular present, Bloom now sees the secular present in the religious future. Already "a Kafkan facticity or contingency now governs our awareness of whatever in Jewish cultural tradition is other than normative":[33] a strong, dark truth indeed.

The license for such prophecy is a statement found in one of Bloom's discussions of Freud which I think would have deeply troubled most critics of Trilling's generation: "Pragmatically, Jewish freedom is freedom of interpretation."[34] Bloom is no deconstructionist, but he certainly advocates a far greater play of interpretation than any of his critical precursors; one would have to go back to Freud himself to find an equally bold reader of what we could call the psychology of rhetoric. Ironically, Trilling, in "Freud and Literature," understood the potential for such literary interpretation in psychoanalysis: "it was left to Freud to discover how, in a scientific age, we might still feel and think in figurative formations, and to create, what psychoanalysis is, a science of tropes, of metaphor and its variants, synecdoche and metonomy."[35] Despite such prescience, however, Trilling never goes as far as Bloom. This is not merely to say that no critic of Trilling's generation ever derived a "psychokabbalistic" or antithetical map of misreadings, though that in itself is evidence of the earlier modesty before the text, the belief in normative or primary procedures of reading. No, Bloom's true extravagance does not lie in his manic will to systematize (which he seems to have outgrown, at any rate) nor even in his imperial use of reference and allusion. But consider this question and response:

> What is a poem *for* anyway? is to me the central question, and by question I mean pragmatically what *is* the use of poetry or the use of criticism? My answer is wholly pragmatic, and therefore unacceptable either to those who call themselves humanists or to those of the supposedly new modes. Poetry and criticism are useful not for what they really are, but for whatever poetic and critical use you can usurp them to, which means that interpretive poems and poetic interpretations are concepts you make happen, rather than concepts of being.[36]

Bloom at his most pragmatic would seem to be Bloom at his least Jewish. Normative deference for the text disappears; the injunction to put a hedge around the Torah is flagrantly disobeyed, and a remarkably Postmodern condition prevails: "There are no texts. There are only ourselves."[37] And this is the point at which the various matters of Judaism, Postmodernism, and *différance* converge. Bloom, following Scholem and reinforced by Yerushalmi, understands how much Judaism as a historical entity is a product of constant internal repression, revision, and rupture. He knows that "The Talmud warns against reading Scripture by so inclined a light that the text reveals chiefly the shape of your own countenance. Kabbalah, like the poetry of the last two centuries, reads Scripture only in so inclined or figurative a defensive mode."[38] He insists that "We do not want the rabbis, or anyone else, to tell us what or who is or is not Jewish. The masks of the normative conceal not only the eclecticism of Judaism and of Jewish culture, but also the nature of the J writer's Yahweh himself."[39] In itself and for itself, Judaism is origin and other, difference and deferral, and Bloom, more than any other Jewish intellectual, has applied that gnosis to the study of literature, undermining the notion of cultural authority which an earlier generation tried so hard to establish.

Yet Bloom is a rueful cultural prophet who offers his vision of the breaking of the vessels only with great reluctance. In his discussion of the cultural prospects of American Jewry, he mourns the loss of what he calls the "text-centeredness" which once distinguished American Jews as an intellectual elite. Without such text-centeredness, "American Jewry, except for the normatively religious, will blend away into the quasi-intelligentsia" because "For many reasons—social, technological, perhaps belatedness itself—it just is becoming harder and harder to read deeply in America."[40]

In the space between Bloom the fierce student of the revisionary self and Bloom the mourner of textual community we find the contemporary Jewish intellectual's ambivalence to the Postmodern. Although I for one do not miss the pretensions of Jewish literary intellectuals to cultural centrality, like Bloom I recognize the seriousness of the loss of text-centeredness which accompanies such claims. To conclude this chapter, I return to the theorists of the Postmodern, this time to Charles Newman and his book *The Post-Modern Aura:*

> ...Post-Modernism represents not so much formal innovation in itself as a change in the dynamic between literature and what might quaintly be described as the social order. It signifies a change in the context into which texts are

received, a recognition that institutions of transmission sub-
stantially alter what is being conveyed, and that institutions
are defined in the contemporary world by their breaking
points.[41]

Jewish literary intellectuals feel this more acutely than any other
group in our culture, for more than any other group they have been
obsessed with institutions of transmission. As we continue to discover the breaking points of which Newman speaks, I can only hope that
this Jewish obsession with cultural transmission survives.

Chapter 2

Harold Bloom; Or,
the Sage of New Haven

As a paradigm for contemporary Jewish writers and intellectuals, Harold Bloom is an especially vexing figure. To be sure, Bloom's notions of Judaism's "text-centeredness" and of its essential understanding of writing as revision are major contributions to Jewish literary thought in our time. Likewise, they are keys to Bloom's own thought, both sources of his vision and crucial proofs of his system. But when it comes to Bloom himself, just what do revision and "text-centeredness" mean? Perhaps such concepts, however convenient, only confirm Bloom's rather perverse insistence that there is no essential distinction between literature and criticism, that "all criticism is prose poetry."[1] As I have already noted, it is assertions such as this, violating all sense of literary "manners," that would have greatly disturbed humanistic critics, including Jewish critics, of the preceding generation: "Professor Moldy Fig," as Bloom likes to typify them. On the other hand, a deconstructionist would ask what all the fuss was about: Bloom's work, more or less unwittingly, merely propels itself into the abyss of language which dissolves all generic distinctions into so much "text." Bloom spends more of his time attacking this trendier attitude, "at best gorgeous nonsense, and at worst only another residuum of the now wearisome perpetual crusade of intellectual Paris against its own upper middle class."[2]

Contrary to appearance, however, Bloom repeatedly insists that he does not come down between these two positions, but rather sees no real difference when comparing them. As he flatly describes himself:

> The interpreter here is a Jewish Gnostic, an academic, but a
> party or sect of one, equally unhappy both with older and
> with newer modes of interpretation, equally convinced that
> say [M. H.] Abrams and Jacques Derrida alike do not aid
> him in reading poems as poems.[3]

The dissatisfaction that Bloom is expressing here has much to do
with his own status as a writer, and hence the relation of academic
criticism to *belles lettres* in our time. Fervently rejecting the consensus
of "an MLA election or a Deconstructive banquet,"[4] speaking more
and more like an Emersonian aphorist or Biblical *nabi,* occasionally
indulging in self-parody but still quite serious in regard to his radically self-reliant Gnostic stance, Bloom continues his sublimely
grotesque amelioration of disciplines and traditions, the textual wandering that is his own belated version of both the Exile and the Fall.
As Jean-Pierre Mileur, one of Bloom's subtlest commentators, points
out:

> The exile that makes meaning possible manifests itself as
> belatedness, and the form of that belatedness, partially
> described by the revisionary ratios, is Bloom's own proce-
> dure of rhetorical substitution—his endless wandering from
> the language of religion, to psychology, to philosophy, to
> rhetoric—which rehearses a similar homelessness, since no
> rhetoric ever actually subsumes and becomes entirely suffi-
> cient to the purposes of any other. Being cut off from the
> substance, from the literal, is the price paid for meaning. But
> this suffering is also the freedom to trope and thus to be
> elsewhere—our defense against the literality of death.[5]

When the narcissistic self is wounded by the inescapable knowledge of its impending mortality, the result in strong writers is the "lie
against time" that is the text. And just as meaning wanders rhetorically and psychically within the text and between texts (hence the
need for a map), so Bloom wanders among the discourses, gloomily
wrestling (despite his apparent high spirits) one author after the next,
like the protagonists of the Gnostic fantasies he so adores. Will
Bloom ever find, to borrow George Steiner's term, a textual homeland—in the minds of his readers, if not his own? Or, if such a question is too benign for such a fetishistically pragmatic, fiercely appro-
priative thinker, what use can we find for this prodigious sage?

Beyond Normative Literary Criticism

> I remember, as a young man setting out to be a university teach-
> er, how afflicted I was by my sense of uselessness, my not exactly
> vitalizing fear that my chosen profession reduced to an incoher-
> ent blend of antiquarianism and culture-mongering.[6]

Despite his honest and wholly understandable ambivalence, Bloom is
now ensconced as an arbiter of culture, and as such is given more to
the mode of confession than most practitioners of an art once quaintly
considered to have had pretensions of objectivity. After Bloom
recounts a personal anecdote (it is invariably charming), he usually
proceeds with an exposition of one or another of his most controversial themes. The implication, confirmed by the pragmatic basis of
Bloom's theorizing, is that personal needs or desires have led him to
his unique literary determinations, a statement which Bloom himself,
as an ephebe of Nietzsche and Freud, no doubt would find rather
banal. However, Bloom's immensely overdetermined revisionism,
with its emphasis on Family Romance and the Will to Power, still does
not automatically account for his insistence that normative literary
criticism must free itself from "the modest handmaiden's role prescribed by the modern Anglo-American academy,"[7] that professors of
literature, in the end, must not merely provide instruction in reading
but must "teach how to live."[8] In *After the New Criticism,* Frank
Lentricchia calls his chapter on Bloom "The Spirit of Revenge," but it
is more than the New Criticism, or even as august a father-figure as T.
S. Eliot that Bloom at his most sincere, most impassioned, and most
cunning seeks to overthrow: it is nothing less than literature itself. If
the deconstructionist seeks to demonstrate that all modes of meaningful discourse can be endlessly deferred because of the ambiguities and
contradictions of language, then Bloom assaults those same modes of
discourse by concentrating instead upon personal power:

> Disabuse yourself of the lazy notion than any activity is disin-
> terested, and you arrive at the truth of reading. We want to
> live, and we confuse life with survival. We want to be kind, we
> think, and we say that to be alone with a book is to confront
> neither ourselves nor another. We lie. When you read, you con-
> front either yourself, or another, and in either confrontation
> you seek power. And what is power? *Potentia,* the pathos of
> more life, or to speak reductively, the language of possession.[9]

To this we can add Bloom's earlier assertion, opposing deconstruction, that "the human writes, the human thinks, and always following after and defending against another human, however fantasized
that human becomes in the strong imaginings of those who arrive
later upon the scene."[10]

When we take such statements—and many more like them—
together, we arrive with Bloom at the lofty solipsism or Gnosis of the
self toward which his dialectics of influence and fascination with
power always lead. More than any other element in his theories, it is
Bloom's Gnosis—"a timeless knowing, as available now as it was
then, and available alike to those Christians, to those Jews and to
those secular intellectuals who are not persuaded by orthodox or normative accounts or versions of religion"[11]—which cancels not only
normative religious practices but normative literary practices as well.
This is not to say that literature of the traditional genres will cease to
be produced (though Bloom always pretends amazement when
another ephebe somehow manages to crawl, like some Kafkaesque
insect, out from under the Oedipal heap of precursors), but that our
perceptions of literary production may come to constitute literature
in a manner that is every bit as psychically potent and aesthetically
charged as the text we read and interpret. For Bloom, this has always
been the case; it is the deep truth of all literary creation. It seems
beside the point to term such understanding, whether derived from
reading or writing, "literary criticism," which is to say, knowledge of a
work that is other than our own. Indeed, we have made the work our
own, having transformed it, through the necessary revisionary ratios,
into Gnosis, which stands apart from all creation, especially the cosmos of all created, anterior texts. As Bloom declares:

> Poetry and criticism are useful not for what they really are,
> but for whatever poetic and critical use you can usurp them
> to, which means that interpretive poems and poetic interpre-
> tations are concepts you make happen, rather than concepts
> of being.[12]

Or to cite one of his favorite aphorisms of Emerson, "for every seeing soul there are two absorbing facts—*I and the Abyss.*"

In *Agon,* the opening chapters of which codify so many of
Bloom's earlier, implicit conclusions, we are informed that unlike
philosophical or rational theological knowledge, "Gnosis never yields
to a process of rigorous working-through."[13] I would argue, howev-

er, that *Kabbalah and Criticism,* often considered the most esoteric of Bloom's works, is the site of just such a working-through, where the revisionist, with his Orthodox upbringing and his equally orthodox New Critical training, teaches himself to go against the Talmudic injunction which he himself quotes and, like the Kabbalists, reads "by so inclined a light that the text reveals chiefly the shape of your own countenance."[14] Paradoxical as it may seem, Bloom's arguments for the defensive warfare of influence, which shatters the autonomy of the discrete text, finally reinstate textual and even authorial autonomy—at least for the strong writers who, having won through to a renewed sense of identity, can only read themselves. Consider the strategies of this passage:

> when you *know* the influence relation between two poets, your knowing is a conceptualization, and your conceptualization (or misreading) is itself an event in the literary history you are writing. Indeed, your knowledge of the later poet's misprision of his precursor is exactly as crucial a concept of happening or historical event as the poetic misprision was. Your work as an event is no more or less privileged than the later poet's event of misprision in regard to the earlier poet. Therefore the relation of the earlier to the later poet is exactly analogous to the relation of the later poet to yourself. The ephebe's misreading of the precursor is the paradigm for your misreading of the ephebe. But this is the relation of every text to every reader whatsoever. The same figures of belatedness govern revisionary reading as govern revisionary writing.[15]

Lentricchia observes that here Bloom is presenting the critic as "one who prefers to 'misread' in order to pump up the value of his own writing."[16] This is undeniable, but I would press the argument further: given Bloom's Gnosticism (in which the initiate, having rejected the created cosmos, recognizes allegiance only to the alien Abyss), the knowledge of the critic in relation to the poet, which is the same knowledge of the poet in relation to the precursor, ultimately establishes the usurping, Oedipal self as the primordial text, no matter how crippling the revisionary wrestling seems to have been. From Satan's deluded "We know no time when we were not as now" to Stevens' perhaps equally deluded "I have not but I am and as I am I am," Bloom's heroes, at their most sublime, speak only about themselves. The map of misreading always seems to lead to the same place, if the reader or writer can endure the entire length of the quest. Bloom warns against idealizing what poems (and presumably, all strong writing) can do for us: interpreting the Lurianc notion of *tikkun* or cosmic restitution, he says:

> Poems cannot restitute, and yet they can make the gestures of restitution. They cannot reverse time, and yet they can lie against time. The Kabbalistic *tikkun* has supernatural ambitions.... We are not theosophists or mystics, and I do not urge another idealizing view of poetry upon us. Pragmatically, representation in belated poetry works to *remind* us of what we may never have known, yet need to believe we have known. Such reminding may be only a lesser kind of restitution, but it does strengthen the mind, almost literally it *re-minds*.[17]

Be that as it may, Bloom's Gnosis of the self can be regarded as immensely gratifying to what remains of our post-romantic sensibility. Bloom promises that we can misread so fiercely, that our delusions can be so artful, that we can become "children of the dawn, earlier and fresher than any completed text ever could hope to be."[18] Perhaps we have discovered that such Gnosis is the one idealized, compensatory restitution that Bloom cannot avoid embracing.

How can Bloom's actual writing be described now that it has steeped in Gnosis for so many years? As we have seen, Bloom claims to be a "sect of one"; he does not care for disciples who will adopt his methods (the same is true of Emerson, as he affirms in his Journal[19]), though presumably he would accept a few, given his belief in the necessity of literary elites.[20] Indeed, it is hard to conceive of even the most audacious and theoretically sophisticated graduate students writing their dissertations in the Bloomian manner; the community of consensus in the persons of their directors would stifle them soon enough, given what the master accurately calls "acceptable critical style": "a worn-out Neoclassical diction, garlanded with ibids, and civilly purged of all enthusiasm."[21] But then, since he tries to dissolve the distinction between literature and criticism, Bloom inevitably looks past the boundaries of academic writing. We may think of him in the company of such strong critics as Kenneth Burke, William Empson, or Northrop Frye and continue to associate his work with that of the now largely dispersed Yale school of criticism. His most recent works, however, reveal the visionary company to which he truly wishes to belong: the Shelley of the *Defense of Poetry*, Pater, Wilde, and of course, Emerson, in all of whose work the language of poetry and the language of criticism can rarely if ever be distinguished.

Bloom goes to some lengths to demonstrate this essential indistinguishability, loftily dismissing normative criticism's emphasis on accurate reading with Wildean wit, and repeatedly citing Emerson to justify their shared belief that "criticism is an art when it does not stop at the words of the poets, but looks at the order of his thoughts and the essential quality of his mind. Then the critic is poet."[22] This statement is similar to Emerson's more famous declaration in *The Poet* that "it is not meters, but a meter-making argument that makes a poem."[23] I cannot argue in the present context how misleading Emerson's remarks of this sort really are, but for now we may note how surprisingly little "wrestling" goes on when Bloom makes use of them. The result is less a misprision than an unquestioning acceptance of the concept, less a deceptively humbling *kenosis* than a prolongation of the precursor's original error. Critics may speak the language of poetry, and in doing so may create a discourse that is insightful, shapely, even, as Bloom would have it, "outrageous." But while it is certainly crucial to study the order of a poet's thoughts, their meter-making arguments, to neglect or even reject the mediating formalisms that make poetry *poetry*—not philosophy, theology, psychology, rhetoric, or any hybrid thereof—is to weaken critics immeasurably, and certainly not to transform them into poets. Emerson compensates for his weak poetry by becoming a wonderfully persuasive master of prose, and at its best Bloom's prose can also rise to the heights. But the insights Bloom provides into the "psychokabbalism" of influence in no way cancel that pragmatic dictum of Ezra Pound, a poet who Bloom frequently enjoys dismissing: "Pay no attention to the criticism of men who have never themselves written a notable work."

Suppose we accept momentarily Bloom's assertion that literary criticism is prose poetry (or that poetry is verse criticism), despite the generic confusion that will result. As I have implied, Bloom is an extremely uneven writer, regardless of how the texts which he produces end up being classified. Large expanses of his prose sound like rough drafts. He proposes searching questions which prove to be rhetorical, as he frequently fails to provide direct answers. He can be obsessively repetitive, yet at the same time appear bewilderingly digressive. The density of quotation, allusion, and simple name-dropping with which the reader constantly must contend can be maddening, regardless if it is approbation or censure which Bloom attaches to each particular citation. And all these leaping figures, these wandering devices, are paraded before us with complete insouciance and utter self-consciousness under the rubric of "wildness" or "extravagance."

These and other similar qualities in Bloom's writing have not escaped notice before. Jean-Pierre Mileur claims that Bloom postpones the inevitable reduction and absorption of his ideas, their domestication into the institutionalized critical tradition, by the dizzying speed and virtuosity of his publication, which gives him a flexibility and capacity for constant self-revision approximating that of orality:

> The frequently heard criticism that Bloom publishes too much too quickly and that his statements are imperfectly consistent with one another clearly amounts to an accusation that he is violating the proper imbalance between the authority of the tradition and the imaginative desire of the individual writer, which the limits of a written tradition and the further difficulties of the institution of publication are intended to enforce.[24]

This almost sounds like a defense of Bloom devised by Derrida and executed by Foucault, and as appealing as *that* fantasy may sound, it remains a fantasy. What Mileur says about publication as an enforcement of institutional standards may apply to a younger, unknown critic, but not to Bloom, whose audience by now is firmly entrenched. In the main, it is an academic audience, which will read his publications whether it relishes or castigates the virtuosity of his style. What Mileur calls the "truly terrifying prospect" of "giving up an assured institutional audience and attempting to form a new one"[25] simply is not a prospect which Bloom will have to face—though he himself probably regards it as rather attractive and not very terrifying at all. Unless at some later date literary theory truly does become the negative theology to which Bloom compares it,[26] he will have to remain, unlike Emerson, not a prophet but a professor of prophecy.

The Agon of Humanism

...reject your parents vehemently enough, and you will become a belated version of them, but compound with their reality, and you may partly free yourself.[27]

But these days, even professors of prophecy have their uses. The unwieldy but willful qualities of Bloom's prose and the generically blurred but urgently voiced argumentation of his project are, both Bloom and his commentators know, agonistically related to the crisis of humanism conveniently represented by postwar modes of Continental thought. With its panoply of sources ancient and modern, Bloom's theory is both a symptom of and a response to this crisis; his Americanized Gnosis, pragmatic and self-reliant, is formulated at least in part as a rejoinder to "all Gallic modes of recent interpretation because they dehumanize poetry and criticism."[28] And while a comprehensive discussion of this crisis, broadly involving questions of the efficacy of scientific knowledge, of the autonomous self, and of the authority of textual traditions, is beyond the scope of any one book, certain of Bloom's formulations go directly to its heart.

Because Bloom and his generation of critics have made even more overt use of religious models of interpretation than their New Critical predecessors, we can say, along with Mileur, that the crisis of humanism focuses in more narrow literary terms upon "the enormously problematical notion of secularization."[29] If the tradition of secular literary culture is threatened by post-structuralist versions of the "human sciences," then Bloom's reappropriations of ancient religious revisionism (Kabbalah, Gnosticism, etc.) can be regarded as a defensive return to origins, an *apophrades* indicating the strong possibility that no definitive break was ever made between sacred and secular textual traditions. As we have observed, Bloom makes no distinction between sacred and secular texts within the confines of his revisionary paradigm; thus he can offer a comparative reading of Freud's *Three Essays on the Theory of Sexuality* and the tale of Jacob and the angel from Genesis, and find in both of them the same vision of "a catastrophe creation, a transference, and a family romance."[30] When a literary critic performs feats of this sort, he is playing for high stakes indeed: against contemporary modes of thought which decenter and reinsert the subject as a counter in various linguistic, political, social, or economic processes, Bloom reasserts the primacy of the individual psyche and the authority of a textual tradition based upon such primacy and capable of defending itself against historical vicissitudes through the uncanny mechanisms of persistent revisionism.

The fact that since the Enlightenment, if not earlier, the authority of sacred texts has been dispersed and only partially redistributed among a series of canons that can be defined broadly as "literary" ultimately makes little difference to Bloom; as Mileur points out, his is an essentialized and ahistorical Gnosis fueled by "his insistence on breaking down the distinction between religion and secularity, which is so constitutive of our sense of ourselves and our activities."[31] Bloom is both an ancient and a modern, or perhaps both a religious and a secular writer, since he responds to the most modern of intellectual predicaments with what many intellectuals today would perceive as the most archaic of stances. That he has put such a figure as Freud in the service of his theory in no way mitigates this circumstance: in order to further the vitality of any text, Bloom, true to his Jewish heritage, must make all things old. When an aggressive Postmodernist like Foucault declares that

> criticism is no longer going to be practiced in the search for formal structures with universal value, but rather as a historical investigation into the events that have led us to constitute ourselves and to recognize ourselves as subjects of what we are doing, thinking, saying...[32]

Bloom only shakes his head, insisting that such a theorist is "massively irrelevant" to literature. Bloom's omnipresent "Scene of Instruction," while it may de-idealize authorial relations, reinstates rather than deconstructs "formal structures with universal value." Although he refuses to be associated with traditional literary humanism as well as deconstruction, since they differ only in regard to "degrees of irony, of the human gap between expectation and fulfillment,"[33] Bloom may still come to be regarded as an exaggeratedly defensive spokesman for humanistic values, who sees in literature not the "antimimesis" of Derridean free play, but the "supermimesis" of eternal psychic struggle, ineluctably stamped upon every text.

Bloom's theoretical system obviously consists of representations of this struggle, and as one might expect, the tradition of literary humanism troubles him deeply, for he must perceive it as a vexingly idealizing precursor to his own more savage vision. Consider these uneasy observations:

> If the imagination's gift comes necessarily from the perversity of the spirit, then the living labyrinth of literature is built upon the ruin of every impulse most generous in us. So apparently it is and must be—we are wrong to have founded a humanism directly upon literature itself, and the phrase "humane letters" is an oxymoron. A humanism might still be

founded upon a completer *study of literature* than we have
yet achieved, but never upon literature itself, or any idealized
mirroring of its implicit categories. The strong imagination
comes to its painful birth through savagery and misrepresen-
tation. The only human virtue we can hope to teach through
a more advanced study of literature than we have now is the
social virtue of detachment from one's own imagination, recognizing always that such detachment made absolute
destroys any individual imagination.[34]

It seems then that literature and humanism are ultimately incompati-
ble, and only a constant policing of the writer's violent imagination and
not its idealized celebration (as in the work of, say, Northrop Frye) will
permit aspiring humanists to continue in their literary education.

Here Bloom both models himself after Freud and swerves away
from him. Bloom distinguishes himself from his mentor in that for
the former, artistic creativity is a matter of repression rather than sub-
limation: "To equate emotional maturation with the discovery of
acceptable substitutes [such as the writing of poems] may be pragmatic wisdom, particularly in the realm of Eros, but this is not the
wisdom of the strong poets."[35] In Bloom's revision of the Freudian
narrative, it is in the id and not the superego that the poetic father-
figures are to be found. Yet Bloom's dark wisdom regarding the savage desires of the strong imagination also resembles Freud's pessimism in such late works as *Civilization and Its Discontents,* in
which the superego is seen as capable of severely punishing an ego
which has already renounced many of its instinctual pleasures. In
Bloom's understanding of literature, the detached "study of literature," or criticism, may operate as a superego, standing over the
"strong imagination," though such critical detachment can also lead
to the destruction of the imagination. As Freud notes, "Every renunciation of instinct now becomes a dynamic source of conscience and
every fresh renunciation increases the latter's severity and intoler-
ance."[36] Against such circumstances, Bloom remains the apostle for
the fierce poetic voice: in his terms, "criticism teaches not a language
of criticism...but a language in which poetry already is written."[37]

Consider, for example, his use of the Hebrew term *davhar*
("word"). Bloom compares it with the Greek *logos:*

The concept of *davhar* is: speak, act, be. The concept of *logos*
is: speak, reckon, think. *Logos* orders and makes reasonable the

context of speech, yet in its deepest meaning does not deal with the function of speaking. *Davhar*, in thrusting forward what is concealed in the self, is concerned with oral expression, with getting a word, a thing, a deed out into the light.[38]

Naturally, Bloom prefers the Hebrew notion, for in contrast to the Greek sense of order and context in *logos*, *davhar* emphasizes linguistic acts of the self that establish the priority of personal being. Although Bloom relates Derrida's kabbalistic sense of language to *davhar*, his general critique of deconstruction (and probably all philosophies derived from Greek models) follows from its continued reliance on *logos*, "word referring only to another word."[39] Genuinely assertive acts of speech are thrust forward by the (obviously phallic) self; they are creative insofar as they emulate the original act of Creation in Genesis. As Bloom well knows, Torah is traditionally understood as *davhar*: as "the concentrated power of God Himself, as expressed in His Name," it is "an instrument of Creation, through which the world came into existence."[40]

There is much to be said for this position, if not from a philosophical than at least from a literary point of view. *Davhar* empowers the speaking self, allowing for a sense of priority—and hence authority—that guarantees a vision of independent life. Thus Bloom can ask of Wordsworth in conjunction with Milton, "what is the Word (*davhar*) of his own, both as against and related to the Word of Milton, that Wordsworth is compelled to bring forward in *Tintern Abbey?*"[41] The same could be asked of all strong writers and their precursors, regardless of whether they are members of Bloom's particular pantheon, for *davhar* specifies individual human relations among texts, however agonistic they might be. The self of the text is never entirely dispersed among linguistic or social practices, and while it resists a communal identity, its agon guarantees it will never be entirely isolated.

The same embattled humanism is apparent in Bloom's various pronouncements regarding contemporary concern over the formation and perpetuation of authoritative literary canons. The subject calls forth some of his most elliptical and gnomic prose, generating numerous digressions and verbal substitutions in an already restless discourse. Bloom first approaches canon formation via the vexed term *tradition*, which he defines as "good teaching, where 'good' means pragmatic, instrumental, fecund."[42] In a later discussion, he first asserts that "we cannot define tradition...and I suggest we stop trying," then shifts to the related term *canonization* and states that "when you declare a contemporary work a permanent, classic achievement, you make it suffer an astonishing, apparent, immediate loss in meaning."[43] What is beginning to emerge is Bloom's great ambivalence toward his subject and hence toward his culturally burdened role of sage: whereas the teaching or passing-down of tradition initially or ideally serves as personal empowerment, it invariably finds itself complicit in the procedures of canonization, which reify or sterilize the text, leaving the teacher's handing-over of fecund knowledge powerless and the student bereft. It is better, then, not to seek to define the process in which we are engaged, but Bloom is temperamentally incapable of following his own advice. From canonization he switches again to his perennial master-trope of *influence,* concluding that

> "influence," substituting for "tradition," shows us that we are nurtured by distortion, and not by apostolic succession. "Influence" exposes and de-idealizes "tradition," not by appearing as a cunning distortion of "tradition," but by showing us that all "tradition" is indistinguishable from making mistakes about anteriority. The more "tradition" is exalted, the more egregious the mistakes become.[44]

When he is most gloomily humanistic, Bloom always consoles himself with notions of distortion and mistakes. Because tradition can never be what we wish it to be, because what we know and value most truly about the text is lost to canonization, then the entire process may as well be viewed as influence anxiety, an endless sequence of psychohistorical caricatures.

And yet somehow the capable self continues to emerge, and strong poems continue to be written:

> A strong poem, which alone can become canonical for more than a single generation, can be defined as a text that must engender strong misreadings, both as other poems and as literary criticism.... When a strong misreading has demonstrated its fecundity by producing other strong misreadings across several generations, then we can and must accept its canonical status.[45]

This tautological definition indicates that, since misreading is the only means through which we can achieve enabling psychological authority, canonization too, despite its enervating effect, may as well be regarded as a wholly pragmatic process. The generative fecundity of strong misreading becomes the final arbiter of cultural value: if the text proliferates through its legible afterlife, then it has won canonic status. Bloom's formulation of canonization may be seen as a darker (or misread) version of Gershom Scholem's, as it appears in "Revelation and Tradition as Religious Categories in Judaism":

> In the process of this renewed productivity, Holy Scriptures themselves are sometimes enlarged; new written communications take their place alongside the old revelation and the tradition. A sort of no-man's-land is created between the original revelation and the tradition. Precisely this happened in Judaism, for example, as the Torah, to which the quality of revelation was originally confined, was "expanded" to include other writings of the biblical canon that had first been subsumed, completely and emphatically, under the heading tradition and considered merely repositories of this. Later, the boundaries often shifted: the canon, as Holy Writ, confronted tradition, and within the tradition itself similar processes of differentiation between written and oral elements were repeated.[46]

For Scholem, this process of expansion, leading to the convention of commentary as the complement of revelation, is the means of providing individual freedom within the bounds of communal and historical authority. Scholem's expanding commentary becomes Bloom's several generations of misreadings: the self in its struggle against anteriority is preserved and remains viable, but, as we have seen before in Bloom's agonistic humanism, the historical, the communal, and the political dimensions recede into the background. In this case, canon formation becomes solely a psychohistorical study, a self-implicating continuum of stronger or weaker personalities.

Even within the bounds of pragmatism, this is a severely limited view. While the study of influence as it develops in Bloom's theory (part Freudian, part kabbalistic, but wholly American) is crucial to an understanding of canon formation, it lacks the political insights that are the necessary complement to any individualistic psychology. If the crisis of humanism is a crisis of cultural authority, and if canons of sacred or secular literature serve as the vehicles for such authority, then Bloom is telling only half the story—for textual power is as much a matter of communal consensus as it is psychic struggle. As Gerald L. Bruns says in his consideration of the Hebrew Scriptures:

> To inquire into the canonization of the books of the Torah is to ask how they came to possess their power over a nation and people. What did it mean for these books to become binding? More important, what were the conditions under which such a thing occurred?[47]

It is symptomatic of Bloom's individualistic ideology that he rarely makes such inquiries, despite his professed concern for literary traditions. And while I think we must respect Bloom's reverence for the heroic voice and its "lie against time," we must also recognize that individual writers, no matter how "strong," draw their strengths at least partly from manifestly social configurations of power. Nor am I deterred by the fact that this statement could be made by either a "traditional humanist" or a "deconstructionist": after all, in the course of Bloom's rhetoric, these figures are straw men; they represent the self-imposed intellectual boundaries within which Bloom has chosen to narrate his belated vision of cultural loss, the Fall from canonic authority, the Exile from the homeland of the text.

Raising the Sparks

From our perspective, religion is spilled poetry.[48]

When Bloom, thinking of Yerushalmi's *Zakhor,* states "that all contemporary Jewish intellectuals are compelled to recognize that they are products of a rupture with their tradition, however much they long for continuity,"[49] his rather mournful tone masks a certain defiance, if not a madcap glee. At about the same time, he also declares that philosophy "is a stuffed bird on a shelf; so, of course, is religion, and they are equally dead and equally stuffed."[50] Given Bloom's enormous appropriations of Jewish thought, one can only conclude that a certain lingering fascination is to be found around that stuffed bird.

Bloom seems to define Jewishness in terms of negation and loss. Obsessed by the endless permutations of Jewish thought and identity since biblical times, yet resolutely opposed to the orthodox and even normative modes of Judaism found today, Bloom is a vivid example of Scholem's assertion that even in an age of secularization, "so many people from opposing camps, such as that of the pious and that of the consciously and emphatically irreligious, nevertheless confess their identity as Jews," making the question of modern Judaism's relation to tradition still one of great moment.[51] For Scholem, and certainly for Bloom, to be Jewish in a modern sense is to problematize Judaism—to wander, to question, to agonize, and to appropriate, like a Kafka, a Benjamin, a Freud. David Biale claims that, for Scholem, "the only possible definition of Judaism is the totality of the contradictory principles which make up Judaism."[52] This is even truer for Scholem's ephebe, since Scholem remains a normative believer, while Bloom, the "Jewish Gnostic," repudiates religion as such. Bloom can still lay claim to Jewish identity because, paradoxically, modern Jewish authority, at least by implication, declares that authority in Judaism no longer obtains.

It is deeply ironic then that if Bloom represents the dilemma of modern Judaism's lack of unified authority, he still gravitates, as if by instinct, to the most archaic aspects of Jewish belief, to those fraught with the strongest imperatives. In his Introduction to Olivier Revault d'Allonnes's *Musical Variations on Jewish Thought,* Bloom reveals his fascination with the book's central vision of Judaism as a nomadic cult moving with the currents of time and opposed to the spatial orientation of state power. This vision accords with Bloom's own understanding of "wandering meaning": his meta-narrative of belated texts parallels the belated condition of diasporic Jewry, and both find their meaning only through nomadic or vagrant existence. Furthermore, Bloom sees the Freudian dynamics as based upon "Jewish myths of Exile" too; thus "psychoanalysis becomes another parable of a people always homeless or at least uneasy in space, who must seek a perpetually deferred fulfillment in time."[53] In short, the social, the psychological, and the literary spheres coalesce around the notion of Exile, as wandering generates meaning and fulfillment is always deferred.

Bloom's most compelling insight in this regard concerns the motivation for literary production within the Jewish tradition of textuality. As he pointedly observes, "In Hebraic tradition, all literary representation partook of transgression, unless it were canonical. But Exile is a profound stimulus to the human anxiety for literary representation."[54] In effect, Bloom explains why Jews have remained the People of the Book. While it is a commonplace in the study of Judaism to observe that the Book replaces the homeland for diasporic Jewry, Bloom notes in addition how the Second Command-

ment is repeatedly circumvented, if not violated, due to the thousands of years of psychohistorical pressure imposed upon the Jewish
sensibility by the conditions of exile. Scholem, in "Revelation and
Tradition," posits "new historical circumstances" as the original
impetus for the development of Oral Torah and the tradition of commentary, including the canon-formulating, protective injunction of
the *Pirke Aboth* to put a hedge around the Torah. In Scholem's analysis, revelation, as encoded in Written Torah, undergoes this elaborate transformation due to what he calls, perhaps disingenuously,
"the spontaneous force of human productivity."[55] In Bloom, this
force, filtered through Freud, becomes the anxiety of influence, a
psychic condition and a condition of textual production perfectly
congruent with wandering and exile. The fear of transgression cannot maintain the imagination within the confines of Holy Scripture;
like Jacob wrestling the angel, the great Hebrew agon about which
Bloom writes so eloquently, Jews must always struggle with precursor texts and win their blessing. This blessing, as befits Revault
d'Allonnes's nomadic people, "achieves a pure temporality, and so
the agon for it is wholly temporal in nature": the text, wherever it
may wander, will be preserved in time.[56]

When we recall that the ubiquitous revisionary ratios apply to
both sacred and secular canons, we can understand why such categories as agon, exile, wandering meaning, and so forth, expand to
become part of Bloom's universal, albeit Hebraic critical machine.
The Yahwist and Blake, Luria and Freud, no matter how remote
from each other historically and culturally, all share the same psychological and rhetorical patterns, resulting in the same *stance*. What
they *know* (gnosis) is the struggle for priority and the strong self in a
text that becomes *davhar*, holding firm against the past and imposing
itself upon the future. This is the only compensation for primal loss,
regardless of who partakes of it. Cynthia Ozick is thus sadly mistaken
when she accuses Bloom of turning literature into an idol; as Bloom
would respond, a weakening process of idealization is at work when
Ozick declares that, in the Jewish view, "there is no competition with
the text, no power struggle with the original, no envy of the Creator."[57] Bloom's conception of Judaism, which, as I have implied, is
an extreme version of Scholem's, disdains any such narrative of continuity and faith: all modes of writing, not merely those of secular literature, are equally "idolatrous"; and any commentary, whether it is
a kabbalistic reading of the Torah or a Wordsworthian reading of
Milton, constitutes a violation or break as much as a simple carrying

over. As we have observed, Bloom is no deconstructionist, but the wanderings of his revisionary system come as close to a deconstruction of Jewish tradition as one might have while still appropriating its salient features.

In *Kabbalah and Criticism,* Bloom makes the following comparison: "Like the Gnostics, the Kabbalists sought *knowledge,* but unlike the Gnostics they sought knowledge in the Book."[58] Mileur comments: "For Bloom, Kabbalism in its more orthodox aspect represents revisionism as the defense of tradition; in its more radical, Gnostic aspect, the Kabbalah represents an attempt to move beyond the tradition to envision something new, something elsewhere."[59] These two passages indicate the simultaneous attraction and repulsion in Bloom's relation to the tradition of Jewish textuality; indeed, he is so profoundly in the grip of these antithetical forces that he has made it an important part of his definition of Judaism. Bloom's Gnostic desire to be elsewhere (which he also sees as the founding desire of all poetry) always pulls him from the supposed continuity of tradition, but because he is wedded to the Book (as is all poetry), he can never truly depart. The result of this ambivalence is Bloom's search for gaps and contradictions, his fascination with the agon, his resistance to all forms of stability, and above all, his paradoxical longing for an authority that will never assert itself as a positive belief. David Biale explains why Scholem was attracted to Kabbalah:

> The Kabbalah itself was an underground movement for revival in Jewish history; yet it accomplished its work by appropriating the normative tradition and transforming it. Because it represented "freedom under authority," the Kabbalah proposed bold and farreaching new interpretations of the tradition without destroying the tradition altogether.[60]

Bloom begins where Scholem ends: Gnosticism, in the demonic purity of its self-knowledge, represents the final interpretive step that undoes all tradition. As I have argued, Bloom will never take that step—neither his audience nor his own critical voice will be transformed or end up "elsewhere"—but instead, Judaism provides the site where Bloom's ambivalence toward the Book is endlessly rehearsed.

If this site appears to consist not solely of Jewish texts but of all texts—since Bloom, beginning as a modest explicator of the British Romantics, now wanders endlessly among the genres and disciplines—it is because he has appropriated the most inventive and most powerful of Jewish interpretive processes and has "decentered" it to suit his own syncretic devices. Arguably, the rhetorical as well as psychohistorical rationale for Bloom's nomadic discourse is not only generally Jewish but specifically midrashic. The endless textual turnings of traditional writers of Midrash provide the critic with a way of moving between texts, for as Bloom himself observes, "Interpretation, *Midrash,* is a seeking for the Torah, but more in the mode of making the Torah larger than in opening it to the bitterness of experience."[61] Bloom is correct when he speaks of enlarging the Torah (or filling in its lacunae), but he is anxiously hedging in his resistance to "the bitterness of experience." "Midrash," according to Barry W. Holtz, "arose as an attempt to keep a sense of continuity between the ancient tradition of the Bible and the new world of Hellenistic Judaism."[62] I would speculate that in a strangely parallel manner, Bloom's midrashic project arises as an attempt to keep a sense of continuity between the ancient tradition of humanism and the new world of Postmodern literary attitudes.

How is Bloom's work midrashic; and how does it allow for continuity, given the overt concern for rupture and crisis both in his own books and throughout contemporary literary theory? Born out of cultural anxiety and, (once again) as Bloom himself knows, partly derived from the alien Platonic tradition,[63] Oral Torah in its midrashic form operates out of a scrupulous textual anxiety as well. James L. Kugel explains:

> a perceived contradiction between passages (for example, two slightly different versions of the same law), or a word that does not seem to fit properly in its context, or simply an unusual word, or an unusual spelling of a word—all of these are the sorts of irregularities which might cause the reader to trip and stumble as he walks along the biblical path; and so over such irregularities midrash builds a smoothing mound which both assures that the reader will not fall and, at the same time, embellishes the path with material taken from elsewhere and builds into it, as it were, an extra little lift.[64]

The truth of the Law is thus to be found through elaborate verbal play; what initially appear to be problems in the text provide opportunities for greater religious insights. The sanction for what appears to modern readers as dizzying intertextuality is the Bible's status as a canonized—that is, closed—text. Once more Kugel offers an analogy:

The basic unit of the Bible, for the midrashist, is the verse: this is what he seeks to expound, and it might be said that there simply is no boundary encountered beyond that of the verse until one comes to the border of the canon itself—a situation analogous to certain political organizations in which there are no separate states, provinces, or the like but only the village and the Empire.[65]

The free movement of the interpretation is circumscribed by canonic authority, a dialectical process that Scholem describes at length in "Revelation and Tradition." Successive generations transform Midrash into Torah; hence the famous Talmudic saying, "Turn it and turn it again, for everything is in it."

But successive generations have also interpreted with progressively greater freedom; in Bloom's terms, participants in the Jewish tradition of commentary have had to become more and more extravagant revisionists. Drawing on Scholem, Bloom speaks of the classic textual dilemma facing the first medieval kabbalists:

> How does one accommodate a fresh and vital new religious impulse, in a precarious and even catastrophic time of troubles, when one inherits a religious tradition already so rich and coherent that it allows very little room for fresh revelations or even speculations? The Kabbalists were in no position to formulate or even re-formulate much of anything in their religion. Given to them already was not only a massive and completed Scripture, but an even more massive and intellectually finished structure of every kind of commentary and interpretation.[66]

Thus arose the revisionary theosophical doctrines which culminate in the catastrophic vision of Isaac Luria, the messianic debacle of Sabbatai Sevi, and thence the popularization of Jewish mysticism in Hasidism. As relatively modern a figure as Nahman of Bratslav (1772–1810), who produced his teachings not only under the internal pressures of a tremendous interpretive tradition but under the increasing external pressures of secularization and the Enlightenment, reaches what his biographer considers an extreme in the freedom of his commentaries:

> But in the extent to which he carries this process, Nahman seems to express a desire to extend this method to its break-

ing point. Almost any association is now possible. He frequently gives the impression of a creative artist straining against the limitations of his medium, and seeking to extend its borders so that he will have room in which to create. In a statement rather surprising for a Hasidic master, he advocates complete freedom in the realm of interpretation, as long as the law remains unaffected...[67]

A creative artist straining against the limitations of his medium: it is a description that could be applied to a contemporary literary theorist as well as an eighteenth-century Hasidic rabbi. Nor is this as great a leap as one might suppose.

Bloom, after all, is a self-proclaimed heir to this tradition, and his project can be regarded as a dramatic, perhaps definitive expansion of the midrashic and kabbalistic stance—what Hegel would call its "*Aufhebung.*" As an idiosyncratic Jewish intellectual, Bloom has overstepped the limits of the canon but has maintained the formal interpretive attitudes of earlier modes of Jewish textuality. In other words, Bloom's audacious interpretations, including his notorious attack on the boundaries between literature and criticism, stem from age-old textual assumptions, such as Rabbi Akiva's "All is foreseen, but freedom of choice is given." All is no longer foreseen in the work of a post-Enlightenment humanist (and even less so in that of a deconstructionist!), but freedom of choice certainly still applies. I am reminded of Walter Benjamin's observation that Kafka "sacrificed truth for the sake of clinging to its transmissibility." For Bloom, even more of a latecomer than Kafka, truth *is* transmissibility and little else. The act of interpretation is its own truth, though it cannot find its own truth except through the anteriority of the text it must interpret.

Bloom's Gnostic revision of Jewish commentary finally leads to what is for me the most significant question posed by his work: what does the appropriation of religious categories for secular and humanistic purposes indicate about the current state of literary culture? Mileur touches upon this problem when he analyzes Bloom's treatment of authoritative religious texts as "poetry," considering such treatment as "a synecdoche for that privileged vantage point from which beliefs are depersonalized into humanistic values." If such is the case, then "literary humanism covertly draws on the resources of religion in order to enforce the primacy of humanistic 'values' over religious beliefs and to separate value from belief and attach it to reason."[68] In the main I think Mileur is correct here: Bloom is obviously a secular humanist rather than a believer, though whether a "Gnostic" humanist values reason any more than normative belief remains an open question. To be sure, Bloom turns religion into poetry, but he is equally guilty of turning poetry into religion. His promiscuous application of the revisionary ratios indicates that, in his reading method and choice of texts, he seeks to determine neither religious belief nor humanistic values; what matters for Bloom is willful choice, the personal authority that comes from "crossing over," and much less the final position where one comes to rest.

Caught between his nostalgic longing for authority and his remorseless education in the ways in which authority undermines and negates itself, Bloom chooses to celebrate the hard-won victories of the *pneuma* (the Gnostic "spark" or soul), though he cannot help but mourn the fact that the uncovering of such victories depends upon the endless examination of the fallen, created self in a literary history that is of the Demiurge's making. Bloom is right to insist on the strength of ancient paradigms: he is his own best example of the way in which a modern, secular humanist seeks, like a Kabbalist, to raise the sparks of the shattered vessels. The sparks consist of nothing less than the texts Bloom interprets—remember, "From our perspective, religion is spilled poetry." Literature has experienced a breaking of the vessels; it must be raised up out of it fallen or spilled religious condition. That this is in itself a profoundly religious process reveals the inescapable double bind in which Bloom is caught; and I would further argue that in this predicament he is an excellent representative of modern literary culture.

A sage is one who knows, but more importantly, a sage is also one who remembers. Although he would probably deny it, Bloom longs for the impossible act of *tikkun* that would restore the entire textual cosmos, an act of criticism above and beyond the mere gestures toward *tikkun* he finds in individual texts. We may say then that Bloom *remembers forward,* and that is what we must expect of our sages as we wander toward what appears to be a post-literate world. Scholem speaks of the messianic idea in Judaism as constantly moving between the restorative and the utopian. I celebrate and mourn the work of Harold Bloom, which is caught forever in that heartbreaking dialectic.

▲

CHAPTER 3

Gershom Scholem
and Literary Criticism

Why, given the eclectic nature of today's literary studies, does Gershom Scholem have so few readers? Or, to phrase the question more precisely, why have so few critics attempted to make use of Scholem's work? The fact that he deals with a difficult and esoteric subject can hardly serve as a reason: difficult and esoteric voices in philosophy, psychology, linguistics, and political science have a siren-like effect on the present generation of readers. Indeed, as a widely acknowledged monument of both historiography and philology, Scholem's work should naturally attract not only traditional literary scholars but theorists too, who continually probe such great edifices in all the human sciences to discover their methodological and epistemological foundations, with all their cracks and flaws. Scholem's expansive studies of Jewish mysticism would seem to invite such treatment, demonstrating, as do those studies themselves, equal measures of criticism and respect. But no: although Scholem single-handedly created the field of modern scholarship in the Kabbalah and with it an ongoing succession of dedicated and assiduous students, the appropriation of any aspect of his endeavors to different intellectual pursuits has been a surprisingly rare event—especially for a thinker whose work, at least for Cynthia Ozick, "envelopes Freud's discoveries as the sea includes its most heroic whitecaps."[1]

A slightly more plausible reason for the infrequent uses of Scholem's discoveries in literary rather than religious studies is the frankly Jewish nature of his investigations, linked, of course, to his lifelong Zionism. In the days when the Anglo-Catholic New Critics held sway, little more would have needed to be said. But today, in the midst of a great reconsideration of Jewish Scriptures, when prominent theorists freely acknowledge the Jewish roots of their work and when, more than ever, Kafka appears as the universal writer of our century, one would think that Scholem would naturally take his place in the critical pantheon. Furthermore, as Joseph Dan observes, "By ruthlessly dedicating himself to the comprehensive study of a historical phenomenon in its fullness Scholem presented a conclusion which is meaningful and relevant to any scholar in any field of study."[2] Scholem's very ruthlessness, his unapologetic emphasis on particularity, is itself worthy of critical consideration.

If the answer lies anywhere, we must look at the current state of literary knowledge; that is, we must consider what we know about interpretation. In the conclusion of "Structure, Sign, and Play in the Discourse of Human Sciences," Derrida states:

> There are thus two interpretations of interpretation, of sign, of play. The one seeks to decipher, dreams of deciphering a truth or an origin which escapes play and the order of the sign, and which lives the necessity of interpretation as an exile. The other, which is no longer turned toward the origin, affirms play and tries to pass beyond man and humanism, the name of that being who, throughout the history of metaphysics or of ontotheology—in other words, throughout his entire history—has dreamed of full presence, the reassuring foundation, the origin and the end of play.[3]

What Derrida describes in this passage is meant to be understood as the universal situation of interpretation in the West: either one remains perpetually aware of the predicament of interpretation as exile or one accepts a home in the homelessness of free play, rejecting the origin that is also the goal. But Derrida's words also have a peculiarly Jewish, even kabbalistic resonance.

As I noted in the Introduction, the condition of Jewish literary activity in the Diaspora parallels the situation of the Jewish people itself. Jewish writing suffers what I call "the exile of the text." Traditionally, commentary and interpretation were meant to bring the student of Talmud or Kabbalah closer to the presence: indeed, the Shekinah, the female emanation of Deity that is said to represent the Jewish people in exile, also refers to "the Divine Presence."[4] For Derrida, we live in a period when we can no longer think of interpretation as leading us to the "ontotheological" experience of presence which we have traditionally desired. Faced with the possibility of passing beyond humanism into the realm of play, we avert our eyes as at the birth of a "monstrosity."[5] For Jewish literary concerns, this means accepting, even celebrating, a condition that is tantamount to permanent exile, a massive disruption of the traditional view of writing and interpretation.

It is at just this point that we can begin to appreciate the importance of Gershom Scholem, who is preeminently a historian and theorist of disruption. Robert Alter calls Scholem a modernist, one for whom "the truth is to be sought in extremes."[6] One has only to consider the titles of some of Scholem's major essays—"Redemption Through Sin," "Revelation and Tradition as Religious Categories In Judaism," "Religious Authority and Mysticism," "Tradition and New Creation In the Ritual of the Kabbalists"—to see how true this is. Here is a genuine dialectician at work, willing to take extraordinary risks in order to accurately gauge the flux of accepted truth and startling, even threatening innovation in a given historical phenomenon.

Alter notes the recurrence of three words in Scholem's discourse: "paradox," "dialectic," and "abyss."[7] These are prized terms in the vocabulary of modern literary criticism, the first dating back to the New Critics, the second a ubiquitous continental import, the third a fashionable invocation to the *deus absconditus* of deconstruction. But despite such discursive similarities, we must never forget that Scholem is primarily an historian: the texts he examines within their historical circumstances are always regarded, however obscure or recondite they might be, as having an ascertainable impact upon specific communities. When Scholem identifies the explosive messianic tensions in the Lurianic Kabbalah, as arcane a theosophical system as can be imagined, he goes on to demonstrate how such forces result in Sabbatianism, perhaps the most important Jewish mass movement since the destruction of the Second Temple. It is difficult to think of such concerns in terms of free play: here at least, interpretation continues to be lived as exile.

The literary critic who has made the most thoroughgoing attempt to come to terms with Scholem's thought is, of course, Harold Bloom. There is a certain irony to be found in this relationship however, since Bloom, even if we grant Frank Lentricchia's remark that "Few have succeeded, as Harold Bloom has succeeded, in returning poetry to history,"[8] is anything but a historical thinker in Scholem's sense of the term. Bloom's own assessment of Scholem deserves to be quoted at length:

> Scholem's massive achievement can be judged as being unique in modern humanistic scholarship, for he has made himself indispensable to all rational students of his subject.... Kabbalah is essentially a *vision of belatedness,* and I would praise Scholem above all for having transformed his own belatedness, in regard to the necessary anteriority of his own ancient subject, into a surprising earliness. Kabbalah is an extraordinary body of rhetoric, and indeed is a theory of rhetoric, and Scholem's formidable achievement is as much rhetorical or figurative as it is historical. In this deep sense, Scholem has written a truly Kabbalistic account of Kabbalah, and more than any other modern scholar, working on a comparable scale, he has been wholly adequate to his great subject. He has the same relation to the texts he has edited and written commentaries upon that a later poet like John Milton had to the earlier poets he absorbed and, in some ways, transcended. Scholem is a Miltonic figure in modern scholarship, and deserves to be honored as such.[9]

As is his wont, Bloom here transforms Scholem into his own precursor; that is, he is creatively misreading Scholem as part of his effort to establish himself as a strong critic in Scholem's line. Still, I think Bloom is correct to speak of Scholem in Miltonic terms and to indicate that Scholem's analysis of Kabbalah renders it accessible to us in terms of rhetoric or figuration as well as history. It is in the field of rhetoric that Bloom has made the most notable use of Scholem, recapitulating the older scholar's numerous accounts of the Lurianic system so that it becomes one set of coordinates for Bloom's huge map of misreading. Kabbalistic adumbrations of movements within the Godhead become analogous to rhetorical turns within the poem, as well as Freudian psychic defenses and "revisionary ratios" between earlier and later poet. Arguably, Bloom *de-historicizes* Scholem's interpretation of Kabbalah, since Scholem always takes pains to search out the connections between mystical developments within a textual tradition and specific circumstances of Jewish communities in which they arise. Thus the Lurianic Kabbalah and its emphasis on "catastrophe creation" cannot be fully understood without reference to the town of Safed and its role as a haven after the traumatic expulsion of the Jews from Spain in 1492. Bloom is certainly aware of this aspect of Scholem's research, but he swerves from it by arguing that the Kabbalists, spurred on by the anxiety of influence, formulated (or discovered) a paradigm for creative misreading, a psychology and a rhetoric that may be found throughout subsequent Western literary traditions. In Bloom's appropriation of Scholem's work, psychic and textual structures, always more amenable to speculative theory, takes precedence over historical spadework.

It is doubly ironic then that critics must follow Bloom's lead in dealing with Scholem while knowing full well that even to attempt to appropriate Scholem's efforts for literary purposes is to misinterpret or subvert them. But this is itself a lesson to be drawn from Scholem's historiography—at least according to Bloom. Cynthia Ozick reports that Scholem's response to Bloom's borrowings was simply to quip "It's a free country."[10] At the risk of making too much of an offhand remark, I believe that this is most revealing: *freedom,* while not a candidate for Alter's list of key words in Scholem's lexicon, is still a crucial concept in his analyses of texts and events. Freedom manifests itself as a desire for creative divergence and novelty in literary expression or religious experience. Its antithesis is an equally strong psychohistorical power, conservative, entrenched, resistant to innovation and suspicious of enthusiasm. But as Scholem declares in "Religious Authority and Mysticism," "A mystic may substitute his own opinion for that prescribed by authority, precisely because his opinion seems to stem from the very same authority."[11] The result, as Derrida would observe, is a perpetually decentered structure in which the source of authority can never be fully located, but instead calls continually for interpretation—the signature of exile. But unlike Derrida, Scholem (and his ephebe Bloom) cannot endorse freedom as post-humanist play. Exile remains exile, a painful "ontotheological" lack for which there is no adequate compensation, including the free play of interpretation. Thus freedom is compelled to contend with authority at every observable historical juncture.

One of Scholem's most crucial insights concerns the form such struggles take in religious—and textual—traditions. Because of his dialectical perspective, Scholem tends to see developments in these traditions as manifestations of the antitheses we have just identified. In "Religious Authority and Mysticism," he poses the textual aspect of the problem as follows: "where the authority is set forth in holy scripture, in documents bearing a character of revelation, the question arises: what is the attitude of mysticism toward such a historically constituted authority?"[12] Scholem's answer demonstrates the simultaneous preservation of authority and assimilation of novelty as the mystic reinterprets the sacred texts. Because of the ancient Jewish view of commentary, which is dependent upon the belief in the revealed scripture's infinite capacity to contain all subsequent interpretations, even the most revolutionary of the mystic's new formulations can be accepted as authoritative by adherents to the faith, despite the obvious appearance of innovation to the investigative historian.

In "Revelation and Tradition as Religious Categories in Judaism," Scholem describes the historical growth of tradition (Oral Torah) as it emerges from the original content of revelation (Written Torah). The expanding interpretative tradition, "the medium through which creative forces express themselves," gradually enters into a process of canonization, but not without serious consequences:

> Tradition is not simply the totality of that which the community possesses as its cultural patrimony and which it bequeathes to its posterity; it is a specific selection from this patrimony, which is elevated and garbed with religious authority. It proclaims certain things, sentences, or insights to be Torah, and thus connects them with the revelation. In the process, the original meaning of revelation as a unique, positively established, and clearly delineated realm of propositions is put in doubt—and thus a development as fruitful as it is unpredictable begins which is highly instructive for the religious problematic of the concept of tradition.[13]

When the creative forces of interpretation become so strong as to vie with the original authority of revelation, Oral Torah comes to be regarded as a preexistent component of Written Torah; thus "revelation comprises everything that will ever be legitimately offered to interpret its meaning."[14] The extraordinary freedom of interpretation demonstrated by one generation of writers after the next is licensed by what Scholem calls "a historical construction whose fictitious character cannot be doubted but which serves the believing mind as a crutch of external authentication."[15] This canonic procedure in effect resolves the contradiction between textual authority and interpretative freedom. Within the verbal community, commentary is seen as a dualistic practice that is simultaneously reverential and presump-

tuous in its relation to the canon, eternally authoritative and historically contingent, measured and spontaneous.

The kabbalistic view of the Written Torah as comprised of an
infinite, braided texture based on the absolute name of God raises
this dialectic of interpretive freedom and canonic authority to a point
of mystical sublimity—and of even greater historical moment. The
original word of God is "meaningless" or incomprehensible; revelation is unique because "it is the very essence of interpretability."[16]
Canonic authority as it is conventionally understood does not exist in
Kabbalah. As Scholem declares:

> Tradition undergoes changes with the times, new facets of its
> meaning shining forth and lighting its way. Tradition,
> according to its mystical sense, is Oral Torah, precisely
> because every stabilization in the text would hinder and
> destroy the infinitely moving, the constantly progressing and
> unfolding element within it, which would otherwise become
> petrified.[17]

"Canon formation" becomes as much a matter of radical change as
authoritative maintenance. Indeed, at its furthest extreme, Kabbalah
asserts that the Ur-Torah, composed by God before Creation in letters of black fire upon white fire, never really finds expression on
earth except through an infinite process of mediation: what we know
as Written Torah is actually Oral Torah, the mediation of a truth that
will remain forever esoteric, incapable of revelation as such.[18] The
monumental text remains with God; tradition from its beginning is a
sequence of creative tropes upon the hidden Word.

This belief in the textual duality of Scripture—what a modern
theorist might call a literary ideology—has a profound affect upon
religious thinkers who find themselves in this tradition, and may even
shed some light on the situation in which critics find themselves
today. As Scholem says of Isaac Luria, whose revisionary Kabbalah
spread widely during the late sixteenth and seventeenth centuries:

> His whole attitude was decidedly conservative. He fully
> accepted the established religious authority, which indeed he
> undertook to reinforce by enhancing its stature and giving it
> deeper meaning. Nevertheless, the ideas he employed in this
> seemingly conservative task were utterly new and seem dou-
> bly daring in their conservative context. And yet, for all their

glaring novelty, they were not regarded as a break with traditional authority.[19]

But the situation of modern critics is not that of Luria: glaring novelty is less easily subsumed by tradition because the study of secular literature, practically by definition, does not lend itself to the establish-
ment of authority in the religious sense of the term. Indeed, in the
present climate, the inevitable fragmentation of literary theory and of
any unified literary canon is accepted and frequently endorsed.

Scholem's subtle interpretation of interpretation has direct
bearing on the problem of such fragmentation, of the indeterminate
center and fictionality of meaning with which contemporary critics
are so concerned. The obvious difference between Jewish religious
commentary and secular interpretative and canonic economies lies in
the fact that secular literature, despite the presences of immensely
authoritative works, is not considered to have emerged as a tradition
based upon revelation. Nevertheless, the concept of freedom in a
productive tension with authority remains a viable one, capable of
informing paradigms of interpretation and canon formation which
neither petrify an exclusive sequence of masterworks nor lose sight of
the undeniably compelling force of the binding text. The writers,
critics and teachers of every generation (all of whom eventually produce commentary of one sort or another) receive or seek for authoritative literature in much the same way as does the kabbalist yearning
for the divine Word. Even when this impulse has been resolutely secularized, revelation continues to operate as a psycholinguistic force
that demands interpretation, emendation, revision—the unfolding,
dialectical process of commentary. What we must realize is that for
"profane" literature, *there is no text that could not potentially constitute "revelation."* Any text or writer can come to be regarded as
authoritative through participation in commentary as a progressive
sequence of literary-historical events. We may now regard as "canonical" that work which functions simultaneously as "Oral Torah" and
"Written Torah," freely troping within an identifiable tradition and
generating variously interpretative texts that would attest to its own
power of "revelation."

Scholem's understanding of these categories and its potential
application to our current theoretical situation may be seen in the
long, combative discussion he held with his friend Walter Benjamin
over the work of Franz Kafka. In a letter to Zalman Schocken,
Scholem speaks of Kafka as one who "walked the fine line between

religion and nihilism." It was this condition in Kafka's work "which, as a secular statement of the Kabbalistic world-feeling in a modern spirit, seemed to me to wrap Kafka's writings in the halo of the canonical."[20] For Scholem, as for Benjamin, there is no question that Kafka is a canonical figure: but what effect does Kafka's borderline state between religion and nihilism have upon the modern understanding of the canonical? Benjamin, as we have seen, notes of Kafka that "his students are pupils who have lost the Holy Writ," a position which, as Anson Rabinbach observes, "is bound up with an irreparable condition of exile which is the (German-Jewish) tradition of modernity."[21] Scholem, however, disagrees: "Those pupils of whom you speak at the end [of Benjamin's essay on Kafka] are not so much those who have lost the Scripture...but rather those students who cannot decipher it."[22] Rabinbach expounds upon this side of the argument as well: "the cosmic exile of the Jews is also an exile from the meaning of the Law, but not from the Law itself."[23]

This, then, is our choice regarding the modern status of canonic literature and, concomitantly, of the activity of interpretation: either the source of textual authority is lost to us, turning interpretation into Benjamin's "untrammeled, happy journey"; or textual authority is present but undecipherable, making interpretation into a ritual performed on the line between devotion and the void. How similar this is to Derrida's two interpretations of interpretations! And long before Derrida, before even Scholem and Benjamin, Kafka himself recognized the dilemma. Writing to Max Brod about their generation of German-speaking Jews, he speaks of how their despair over their confused identities became their inspiration, and proceeds to sketch out a number of "linguistic impossibilities":

> The impossibility of not writing, the impossibility of writing German, the impossibility of writing differently. One might also add a fourth impossibility, the impossibility of writing (since the despair could not be assuaged by writing, was hostile to both life and writing; writing is only an expedient, as for someone who is writing his will shortly before he hangs himself—an expedient that may well last a whole life).[24]

It is out of these impossibilities, preeminently the conditions of writing in exile, that comes the uncanny doubling of pious commentary and modernist innovation which Scholem and Benjamin attempted to codify and which has since been passed down to all their heirs—if the notions of "passing down," of inheritance and tradition, were not themselves of issue! Thus our most influential critics today seem almost temperamentally incapable of remaining simple exegetes; it is impossible for them to write in the way that was traditionally expected of them. But it is equally impossible for them not to write, as the texts to which they are so devoted continue to demand a response.

I have been arguing that Scholem's work can be useful for a theoretical understanding of literary criticism (the interpretation of interpretation) and for the more practical act of reading as well. Individual texts cast light upon the tradition in which they are contained, but also must be regarded as products of determinable currents in that tradition. Here then is an exegesis of one particular poem—Wallace Stevens' "Large Red Man Reading" (1948)—in which I attempt to employ the critical principles I have derived from Scholem's notions of tradition and textuality. Surprisingly little has been written about this poem, even by those critics who have moved through Stevens' entire canon, what the poet calls in *The Auroras of Autumn* (1947) "that crown and mystical cabala."[25] Even in his encyclopedic study of Stevens, Bloom offers only a paragraph on "Large Red Man Reading," and while he identifies a precursor text from Emerson, he overlooks (or represses) a great deal that is more directly kabbalistic—or should I say Scholemesque? At any rate, here is the poem:

> There were ghosts that returned to earth to hear his
>   phrases,
> As he sat there reading, aloud, the great blue tabulae.
> They were those from the wilderness of stars that had
>   expected more.
>
> There were those that returned to hear him read from the
>   poem of life,
> Of the pans above the stove, the pots on the table, the
>   tulips among them.
> They were those that would have wept to step barefoot
>   into reality,
>
> That would have wept and been happy, have shivered in
>   the frost
> And cried out to feel it again, have run fingers over leaves
> And against the most coiled thorn, have seized on what
>   was ugly

And laughed, as he sat there reading, from out of the
    purple tabulae,
The outlines of being and its expressings, the syllables of
    its law:
Poesis, poesis, the literal characters, the vatic lines,

Which in those ears and in those thin, those spended
    hearts,
Took on color, took on shape and the size of things as
    they are
And spoke the feeling for them, which was what they had
    lacked.[26]

The figure of the reader is a familiar one in Stevens. He is the
Emersonian scholar, poet or rabbi, whom Stevens describes, as Bloom
points out, as "the figure of a man devoted in the extreme to scholarship, and at the same time making some use of it for human purposes."[27] Already in this quote from Stevens' letters, we can sense the
tension between abstract knowledge and material use that symbolically charges the images of the poem, especially that of the large red man
himself. If he is in this sense a rabbi, then he looks back to others in
Stevens' poems, especially the "rose rabbi" who appears at the end of
"Le Monocle de Mon Oncle" (1918), pursuing "the origin and
course / Of love."[28] In *Notes Toward a Supreme Fiction* (1942), the
rabbi, "grown furious with human wish,"[29] announces the messianic
coming of the imagination's "major man" in his various forms. And
in *The Auroras of Autumn* he is called upon to read "the phases of
this difference," "an unhappy people in a happy world."[30]
    The rose rabbi or large red reader is thus a figure of imaginative
desire who understands and shares in the inadequacy of the human
condition, but at the same time studies a disinterested creation. The
conjunction of the two states produces "the poem of life" inscribed
on "the great blue tabulae." In reading the poem he has written
(which is, self-reflexively, the poem by Stevens himself which we
read), the large red man attempts to theurgically unite cosmic scholarship and human longing in accordance with "the outlines of being
and its expressing, the syllables of its law." Indeed, the red man reading from the blue tabulae, the rabbi reading from the law, is in itself a
symbol of theurgical union.
    The ghosts that return for this reading also have appeared in
Stevens before and, like the large red man, are caught up in the work's

dialectic of symbolism. Their most important role prior to this one has been in the magnificent last canto of *Esthétique due Mal* (1944):

> The greatest poverty is not to live
> In a physical world, to feel that one's desire
> Is too difficult to tell from despair. Perhaps,
> After death, the non-physical people, in paradise,
> Itself non-physical, may, by chance, observe
> The green corn gleaming and experience
> The minor of what we feel.[31]

In "Large Red Man Reading" their desire gets the better of them, and the ghosts return from their metaphysical paradise, "the wilderness of stars," to experience the unstable union of "the literal characters" (literal meaning both material and abstractly textual). The ghosts are all metaphysical desire, which is, in the earlier poem, "the minor of what we feel." But as poignant as Stevens' lines may be, these dead cannot "step barefoot into reality," except in the symbolic sense of their coming back to life in the text. Even the pots and pans have more "reality" than they do, though strangely enough, these objects move in the opposite direction when the poet invokes them, becoming more ghostly and thus more symbolic. (Pots and pans in a Stevens poem are not the same objects as they are in a poem by Williams, his great contemporary and poetic complement.) As for the ghosts, they can find solace in symbolic language alone; only in the discourse of the poem can purely spiritual desire manifest itself in the material world.

Such *poesis* or "making" is akin to kabbalistic ritual, for as Scholem frequently notes, religious observance among the kabbalists is tranformed from rites of remembrance or sanctification to "ritual action [which] not only *represents,* but also *calls forth* this divine life manifested in concrete symbols."[32] And while it is unlikely that Stevens thinks of *his* poem as the same calling forth as performed by the magisterial reader and his purple (that is, kingly) tabulae, "Large Red Man Reading" still acts upon us as does a ritual: we are brought closer to "reality" by an act of the imagination; which is to say, we are provided with a deeper understanding of the interpenetrations of desire in human existence, learning why we are "an unhappy people in a happy world."

Moving from an exegesis of Stevens' poem to a metacritical consideration of this exegesis provides a further consideration of Scholem's relevance to literary criticism. Like Bloom, I must account for establishing what some would consider an arbitrary and willful correspondence between modern poetry and Kabbalah. Bloom's answer is psychoanalytic and rhetorical: the psychic stance of the kabbalists created a precedent followed by other literary traditions, producing "analogous images, tropes, psychic defenses, and revisionary ratios."[33] To this answer I would add the crucial historical element which Scholem uncovers in his analysis of authority and originality.

I have just proposed that the one important difference between Stevens and his large red man is that the former probably regards the theurgy of the latter as a "supreme fiction," a metaphor or symbol for psychic states with which we must contend in the here and now. The same is true for the mythic emanations and interpenetrations of spiritual and material worlds and their various plottings in kabbalistic texts: unlike Yeats or Robert Duncan, Stevens does not consider poems as incantations in the kabbalistic sense, despite the obvious propensity for visionary pronouncements in so much of his work. As he calmly states in "Final Soliloquy of the Interior Paramour" (1950), "We say God and the imagination are one."[34] However, that the gestures in a poem like "Large Red Man Reading" may be seen as analogous to kabbalistic ideas demonstrates Scholem's dialectic of tradition and new creation. Scholem tell us that in their relationship to tradition, mystics such as the kabbalists "are always striving to put new wine into old bottles," since the outer form of belief or ritual is preserved while the inner content undergoes revision.[35] The same is true of Stevens and his poem. An uncanny feeling of authority hovers about such pieces; but if we step back from the text, placing between what Scholem calls "dialectical distance...identification and distance together,"[36] we also become aware of the dissolution of this aura as the poem transforms itself into a novel utterance. It stands both within and apart from tradition; like the ghosts who can only find solace in the symbolic language of the tabulae, the poem can only find solace in itself as a verbal representation of traditional authority. But this, paradoxically, is its new power, a power of pathos to which we as modern readers respond.

Some may regard this view as nostalgic, a pure expression of living what Derrida labels "the necessity of interpretation as an exile." And perhaps it is true that, as Terry Eagleton puts it, tradition "is nothing other than a series of spasms or crises within class history itself...not the scattered letters of an invisible word."[37] Nevertheless, nostalgia for such scattered letters is an ineluctable quality of literary criticism: like Stevens in *Esthétique du Mal,* we study the nostalgias, some of us with greater dialectical distance than others. Such are the kabbalistic insights which Scholem can provide.

▲

CHAPTER 4

The Struggle for Historicity: Cynthia Ozick's Fiction

> Now, as then, it would appear that even where Jews do not reject history out of hand, they are not prepared to confront it directly, but seem to await a new, metahistorical myth, for which the novel provides at least a temporary modern surrogate.[1]

Cynthia Ozick assures her readers that a literature which maintains the Covenant and resists the idolatry of art will approach the liturgical, in which may be heard "a choral voice: the echo of the voice of the Lord of History." Furthermore, "when a Jew in Diaspora leaves liturgy...literary history drops him and he does not last."[2] The self-conscious Jewish writer who remembers, who maintains an awareness of history against the blandishments of the momentary and the immediate, in turn will be remembered, will become a part of (at least Jewish) literary history. Such has been the case throughout the *Galut:* "the tales we care for lastingly are the ones that touch on the redemptive," and such endurance only comes from the moral seriousness of covenanted writing.[3]

Granted that it is always a struggle to maintain the Covenant, Ozick's formulation, which has been developing for many years, is strangely simple: acknowledge the distinction between the Creator and the Creation, and the "Riddle of the Ordinary," inasmuch as it can be answered, will become clear. The imagination, which delights in the endless plenitude of the existent, will recall that all such blessings come from a single Source. The imagination will be endowed with memory and judgment. The imagination will be steeped in history.

But could it not be argued that Ozick's covenanted historical imagination is really ahistorical? As a religious formulation, its understanding of history as the temporal flux of circumstance finally is posited upon an event that is beyond history, located at the end of time. It is true that in Judaism, as Gershom Scholem notes, redemption "takes place publicly, on the stage of history and within the community."[4] But even in Judaism, the most historically conscious religion, "the Kingdom of God," as Walter Benjamin observes, "is not the *telos* of the historical dynamic; it cannot be set as a goal. From the standpoint of history it is not the goal, but the end."[5] These words, more severe than even the strongest of Ozick's polemics, present a serious challenge to the concept of a liturgical literature, a Jewish fiction that can maintain both its redemptive potential and its historicity. Perhaps the entire fiction-making enterprise, in that it partakes of historical contingency, is antithetical to the redemptive promise of God's Covenant with the Jewish people. This could be as great a source of anxiety to Ozick, the normative Jew with a forbidden lust for the magic of narrative, as the idolatry of art she so frequently attacks. Not only does fiction demand an idolatrous devotion to aesthetics, it also demands an engagement with the profane stuff of history that may lead it far from the redemptive quest which Ozick imposes upon it. Benjamin's resolution of this dilemma is, I believe, extremely important in understanding the historical dimension of Ozick's art:

> just as a force can, through acting, increase another that is acting in the opposite direction, so the order of the profane assists, through being profane, the coming of the Messianic Kingdom. The profane, therefore, although not itself a category of this Kingdom, is a decisive category of its quietest approach.[6]

Thus Ozick's career can be understood as an ongoing struggle to secure a sense of historically derived authenticity: in its devotion to history, the essentially profane, even idolatrous work of fiction becomes a Messianic counterforce.

But how can one be assured of the work's historicity? "The true image of the past flits by," writes Benjamin. "The past can be seized only as an image which flashes up at the instant when it can be recognized and is never seen again."[7] Such "moments of danger," surely recognizable by the novelist as well as the critic or historian, inspire much of Ozick's fiction. Since the Jewish writer must respond to history as proof of her faith, since she must shape her observations of the past and present into interpretable meaning, then she must continually devise strategies to capture the true image of the past. Despite her endlessly contradictory statments concerning the purposes of literature, Ozick should be taken at her word when she declares that "*What literature means is meaning*"—at least in regard to the literature that she herself has produced.[8] Though she is haunted by doubt of the final worth of even her most historically responsive stories, Ozick is impelled to produce, in Benjamin's term, "constellations" which join contemporary reality with the historical conditions which produced it. For the tale to have meaning, and consequentially a redemptive potential, it must have historical resonance; like Benjamin's criticism or Scholem's historiography, it must "rub history against the grain." Against what historical matter must the tale resound? In reading Ozick's work, I seek, if not what Fredric Jameson calls its political unconscious, then at least its historical unconscious. I seek not an ideological critique per se, but a redemptive critique that will still take ideology into account.

Consider *Envy; Or, Yiddish in America*. Historicity in Ozick's work often is felt through the crucial dialectic of marginality and centrality; and nowhere is this social dynamic more poignantly apparent than in the modern situation of Yiddish language and literature, especially in America. The pathetic comedy of Ozick's novella presents the Yiddish writer as isolated, bereft of audience, insanely jealous, and desperate for a translator who will bear him into the memory of his people. As Yiddish literature is marginalized, leaving only Ostrover, the "modern" writer who "speaks for everybody," Edelshtein, Ozick's obsessed protagonist, must face the loss of historicity that comes with the loss of language and community. This loss is compounded by the fact that Yiddish has not died a natural death. As the brooding Edelshtein puts it, "And the language was lost, murdered. The language—a museum. Of what other language can it be said that it died a sudden and definite death, in a given decade, on a given piece of soil?"[9] Horror and guilt as well as envy and self-pity motivate Edelshtein's mad acts, which in turn produce some of Ozick's most extravagant prose, the whirlwind of internal letters, monologues, and dialogues in her protagonist's tortured consciousness. Ironically, Edelshtein's Yiddished English, so magically convoluted in the midst of Ozick's energetic narration, seems less like a ghost than a vital force, a survivor in spite of itself.

This then is Ozick's gambit: to transform linguistic exhaustion and the dregs of emotion into a new literature, a New Yiddish which maintains strong rhetorical as well as cultural links with the Old. Edelshtein's epiphany in the midst of his violently climactic argument with Hannah is perfectly appropriate, given the dialectical logic that controls the movement of Ozick's plot, and not in this tale alone:

> He saw everything in miraculous reversal, blessed—everything plain, understandable, true. What he understood was this: that the ghetto was the real world, and the outside world only a ghetto. Because in actuality who was shut off? To whom, in what little space, did God offer Sinai? Who kept Terach and who followed Abraham? Talmud explains that when the Jews went into Exile, God went into exile also. Babi Yar is maybe the real world, and Kiev with its German toys, New York with all its terrible intelligence, all fictions, fantasies. Unreality.[10]

Nowhere else in Ozick's fiction is her understanding of cultural identity and hence of historical endurance more precisely articulated than in this starkly dialectical turn. For the Jewish writer—for Jewish culture itself—historicity is to be gained through the renunciation of active historical life:

> suppose it turns out that the destiny of the Jews is vast, open, eternal, and that Western Civilization is meant to dwindle, shrivel, shrink into the ghetto of the world—what of history then? Kings, Parliaments, like insects, Presidents like vermin, their religion a row of little dolls, their art a cave smudge, their poetry a lust...[11]

The so-called universality of great art, as exemplified by Ostrover's success, becomes a sham in Edelshtein's eyes; only the Covenant and the liturgical art by which it is served can provide authentic meaning to Jewish existence. Edelshtein clings to his Jewish difference, but because Yiddish is now a lost language even among Jews, he must remain forever agonized by his failure to be translated.

The extent to which Edelshtein is Ozick's spokesman is debatable; my guess is that his position is an exaggerated, almost clownish version of Ozick's own. Nevertheless, the point is maintained and often underscored in Ozick's essays: "Western Civilization" cannot sustain and actually may be antithetical to Jewish culture; as we have seen, the only Jewish literature that lasts is that which "touches on the liturgical" or the "redemptive." *Touches on* such religious ground—but does not dwell therein. For despite her distaste for the aestheticism and paganism of Western culture, Ozick also knows that

> Literature, to come into being at all, must call on the imagination; imagination is in fact the flesh and blood of literature; but at the same time imagination is the very force that struggles to snuff out the redemptive corona. So a redemptive literature, a literature that interprets and decodes the world, beaten out for the sake of humanity, must wrestle with its own flesh and blood, with its own life.[12]

This wisdom (derived in part from Harold Bloom) forces Ozick into a paradoxical position, but fortunately, as a writer of fiction she is spared the necessity of logical consistency. Rather, the paradoxical struggle of imagination and faith that for Ozick is the unique mark of the liturgical writer provides the thematic drive for much of her best work. Thus in Edelshtein's epiphany, the "miraculous reversal" of ghetto and outside world which guarantees the purity of his Jewish imagination and his disappearance from history produces in turn a great longing for the security and creative potential of Jewish communal life. For Edelshtein, of course, the destruction of a geographical community coincides with the destruction of his linguistic community. For Ozick, the Judaism of the American Diaspora can a produce a new Yavneh, where Jews will speak and write a New Yiddish.

Ozick's desire for a New Yiddish can be understood as a special, richly productive kind of nostalgia. Ozick longs for a shtetl—cultural and linguistic if not geographical—in which the countervailing forces of imagination and redemption inhabiting the soul of the Jewish writer can most fruitfully work, one upon the other. This shtetl of the soul will afford the Jewish writer her greatest chance to secure the historicity that a figure like Edelshtein has apparently lost. Traces of this nostalgia can be seen whenever Ozick's protagonists attempt to synthesize an imaginative invention drawn from Western culture (or what Ozick in her harsher moments would call an idol) with a Jewish vision of redemption. The failure of all these attempts proves Ozick's contention that any synthesis of imagination and faith will be essentially unstable. But the saving irony is always found in the telling of the tale; in narrative we can *touch on* the redemptive through the exuberance and delight of unfolding events. As in the tradition of Jewish textuality known as Aggadah, the imagination joyfully puts itself in the service of the Law.[13]

The first critic to invoke Aggadah in relation to secular literature was Walter Benjamin in his consideration of Kafka. His remarks, originally contained in a letter to Gershom Scholem, are worth quoting at length:

> Kafka's work presents a sickness of tradition. Wisdom has sometimes been defined as the epic side of truth. Such a definition stamps wisdom as inherent in tradition; it is truth in its haggadic consistency.
>
> It is this consistency of truth that has been lost. Kafka was far from the first to face this situation. Many had accommodated themselves to it, clinging to truth or whatever they happened to regard as truth and, with a more or less heavy heart, forgoing its transmissibility. Kafka's real genius was that he tried something entirely new: he sacrificed truth for the sake of clinging to its transmissibility, its haggadic element. Kafka's writings are by their nature parables. But it is their misery and their beauty that they had to become more than parables. They do not modestly lie at the feet of the doctrine, as the Haggadah lies at the feet of the Halakah. Though apparently reduced to submission, they unexpectedly raise a mighty paw against it.[14]

Arguably, what Benjamin saw in Kafka's work was the inevitable transformation of the Jewish literary sensibility following the Haskalah. This "sickness of tradition," in which the imagination as a vessel for the transmission of (religious) truth finds itself drained of content and even opposed to the Law, becomes paradigmatic for the secular Jewish writer in the modern age. It may well be that the tension between Aggadah and Halakah has always prevailed; one scholar notes that when we consider the two modes, "We are in the presence of the permanent human agon between restraint and freedom.... They are an articulation of the fundamental, universal, interminable combat of obedience and individual conceit."[15] Such a description certainly augments Benjamin's analysis: in the past, the tension between restraint and freedom was found within a carefully guarded religious tradition, but in the work of a modern writer like Kafka, the

boundaries of tradition have been broken and this tension deter-
mines the nature of the text to an even greater extent.

Here is the necessary theoretical means for an understanding of
Ozick's cultural nostalgia. Ozick wishes to bypass the modern gulf
between Aggadic transmissibility and Halakhic truth content, returning to a traditional situation in which the Jewish narrative propensity
does indeed lie modestly at the feet of the doctrine. That such a situation may never have really existed, and that the post-Enlightenment
Jewish author may be the heir to a "permanent human agon" that is
exacerbated by the conditions of secular literary production—this is
the knowledge against which Ozick must defend herself. In a recent
interview, she offers a new perspective on the problem, one in which
faith and imagination can be reconciled:

> I no longer think of imagination as a thing to be dreaded.
> Once you come to regard imagination as ineluctably linked
> with monotheism, you can no longer think of imagination as
> competing with monotheism. Only a very strong imagina-
> tion can rise to the idea of a non-corporeal God. The lower
> imagination, the weaker, falls into the proliferation of
> images. My hope is some day to be able to figure out a con-
> nection between the work of monotheism-imagining and the
> work of story-imagining. Until now I have thought of these
> as enemies.[16]

In the shtetl of her soul, Ozick spins out her extravagant tales, a
remote literary descendent of Rabbi Nachman of Bratslav, who took
to telling stories to purify the imaginations of his disciples in prepara-
tion for the messianic redemption. And while Ozick certainly is not
caught up in any messianic strivings (*The Messiah of Stockholm* can
actually be read as a new version of the rabbinical warning against
"pressing for the end"), she does long for a humanistic literature of
redemption, which, unlike the work of Kafka or Bruno Schulz,
would honor the virtues of the Law in the proper fashion of normative Judaism.

Ozick's troubled defense of what could be called the problem
of modern Aggadah has a telling effect on the overall generic contours of her work, as well as the shape of her plots and the growth of
her characters. Over the course of her career, Ozick zigzags between
a relatively straightforward realism and a benignly magical fabulation.
The latter work usually takes the form of the parabolic tale variously

developed by Kafka, Schulz, Singer and Malamud. Obviously these are very different writers in certain respects, but all of them, I believe, are Aggadists whose parables raise mighty paws against the Halakah. It is here that Ozick swerves from her precursors, for in the main her tales subordinate themselves to established or normative beliefs—no vexed Kafkan paradoxes, no Schulzian arabesques, and relatively few of the narrative ambiguities of Singer or Malamud. As Bloom observes, "So decisive a denial of rupture must be honored as the given of her fiction."[17] Ozick's genius and originality lie in the ferocity of her denial, in the insistence of the tale's subordination to the Law. Strangely, her stories take on their own life—that is, imaginatively vie against the Law—in their stubborn devotion to the traditional Aggadic role and their stubborn linearity of plot and character.

Linearity—or to use a stronger term, predictability—is found throughout Ozick's fiction; and it is a direct result of her concern with the tension between imagination and faith, Aggadah and Halakah. Quick to voice her humanistic protest against "the fated or the static" in fiction, insistent in her belief that the moral of a well-made parable does not appear in the tale but *is* the tale, that "the tale is its own interpretation," Ozick nevertheless produces stories with a powerful sense of the fated, in which the moral appears to have been inserted into and is not embodied by the text.[18] *Puttermesser and Xantippe,* one of Ozick's most explicitly Aggadic works, is a good example. The outlines of the golem narrative are worked out for Ozick in advance, of course, but arguably, one of the reasons that Ozick is attracted to the legend in the first place is its profoundly (and for a Jewish tale, untypically) fated plot structure.

Because Ozick has a great love of the normal and regards the ordinary as permeated with a divine meaning to be endlessly blessed by the "observant" Jew, she also places her faith in the virtues of community and civic life. As represented by Ruth Puttermesser, the diligent lawyer and civil servant, this faith is capable of transforming the beloved but fallen city of New York into an earthly paradise. Puttermesser, no mystic but a rabbinic rationalist, creates the golem Xantippe, who in turn produces the miraculous "*PLAN* For The Resuscitation, Reformation, Reinvigoration & Redemption Of The City Of New York" which enables her creator to become the city's most enlightened mayor. These events, presented through some of Ozick's most lively and balanced comic prose, offer a brighter alternative to Edelshein's gloomy vision of Yiddish in America. The

American-born Puttermesser, who in an earlier story had to invent an Old World uncle for herself, now believes that Jewish civic life in Europe was the precursor of a communal Jewish success story in the United States:

> The Great Rabbi Judah Loew had undertaken to create his golem in an unenlightened year, the dream of America just unfolding, far away, in all its spacious ardor; but already the seed of New York was preparing in Europe's earth: inspiration of city-joy, love for the comely, the cleanly, the free and the new, mobs transmuted into troops of the blessed, citizens bursting into angelness, sidewalks of alabaster, buses filled with thrones. Old delicate Prague, swept and swept of sin, giving birth to the purified daylight, the lucent genius, of New York![19]

We all know the end of this tale, of course: the golem, Puttermesser's instrument of civic redemption, finally proves her undoing; street crime and bureaucratic corruption return as the golem goes on a sexual rampage among the mayor's carefully chosen new administrators. Sexuality is always a reminder of our mortality: Puttermesser, longing for daughters, first creates the golem when she is dumped by her lover Rappoport, whose later fling with Xantippe inaugurates New York's return to its fallen state. As Puttermesser unmakes the spell that binds Xantippe to life, the following dialogue ensues between the hounded mayor and her previously mute factotum:

> The fifth circle was completed; still the golem went on bleating in her little bird's cry. "Life! Life! More!"
> "More," Puttermesser said bitterly, beginning the sixth circle. "More. You wanted more and more. It's more that brought us here. More!"
> "You wanted Paradise!"
> "Too much Paradise is greed. Eden disintegrates from too much Eden. Eden sinks from a surfeit of itself."[20]

Here is yet another reason for Ozick's attraction to the golem legend: because it is, on one level, a cautionary tale about the desire for perfection and the limits of human creativity, it can also serve as a narrative vehicle for Ozick's study of the historical validity of the civic ideal. *Puttermesser and Xantippe* is Ozick's most political work to date—political in the original sense of the *polis*. But as a Hebrew rather than a Hellene, Ozick cannot put her full faith in the human affairs of the polis; she understands that even our most admirable communal aspirations—the very stuff of history as it is usually understood—inevitably unmake themselves. Even Jewish justice and Jewish reason are inadequate bulwarks against lust, greed, ambition, and pettiness. The well-intentioned Puttermesser plays her part in the city's history (at one point she counts all of her predecessors, up to and including Ed Koch), learning too late what Ozick and the reader knew all along: that she and her golem, as historical instruments, are doomed to failure and decreation.

Puttermesser's lesson involves both the representation of historical processes in the fiction of a Jewish writer and the shaping of that fiction by historical processes. If I may resort to Robert Scholes' useful distinction, the former is a matter of *interpretation* while the latter is a concern of *criticism*—and as such, they are relevant not only to *Puttermesser and Xantippe* but to all of Ozick's work.[21] Our desire to understand the tragicomic failures which Ozick so frequently depicts leads us to *interpret* the view of history which emerges from her tales: a view of history as a struggle not merely for the temporally appropriate, but for temporal fulfillment or even blessing, what Harold Bloom, in his various discussions of the agon in the Hebrew Bible, calls *olam* or "time without boundaries."[22] Ozick's protagonists are invariably denied such fulfillment; modern history especially is regarded as a time when passionate Jewish personalities would do better to live quietly under normative patterns of belief, as argued, for example, in the great cautionary tale "The Pagan Rabbi." This recognition leads to a sense of "some deficiency in the text or excess in the reader," and hence to *criticism*.[23] Why does Ozick, who argues strongly for a historically engaged art of fiction, continually produce what appear to be Aggadic parables devoted to (the God of) redemptive history, but which may be read contradictorily as dark shrines to those forces which fatally limit human agency on the historical stage? It is a question reserved for Ozick as opposed to any of her precursors, for she is unique among the writers of this modern Aggadic tradition in insisting that art must be an either/or proposition: *either* liturgical, historically redemptive, and monotheistic *or* aesthetic, blithely forgetful, and idolatrous. For Jewish writers at least, confronted with "the Mosaic revolution in human perception," "There is no Instead Of."[24]

If the contradictions which we meet in reading Ozick emerge, as I have been arguing, from her problematic orientation to history, then what is necessary for both our interpretive and critical tasks is insight into the Jewish self-understanding of history. Yerushalmi's *Zakhor* provides us with just such insight. As Yerushalmi demonstrates throughout his brooding survey, history in the modern sense of a rational analysis of the past stands peculiarly at odds with the traditional Jewish relationship to the past through memory. In the Bible, "It is above all God's acts of intervention in history, and man's responses to them, be they positive or negative, that must be recalled."[25] "Historiography," Yerushalmi continues, "is but one expression of the awareness that history is meaningful and of the need to remember, and neither meaning nor memory ultimately depends upon it."[26] In the post-biblical period, the Jews inherit what they believe to be a "revealed pattern of the whole of history"; thus the normative attitude toward the past, especially for the Rabbis, becomes "an ongoing exploration of the meaning of the history bequeathed to them, striving to interpret it in living terms for their own and later generations."[27] With few exceptions, this religious, memory-based attitude toward the past dominates Jewish culture up until the Haskalah in the late eighteenth century and the subsequent movement to uncover Jewish history in the modern manner called the *Wissenschaft des Judentums.*[28] Only at this point, as Yerushalmi says, "do we really find, for the first time, a Jewish historiography divorced from Jewish collective memory and, in crucial respects, thoroughly at odds with it."[29]

It is within these circumstances, so completely "the product of rupture" (as understood by both Yerushalmi the historian and Bloom the literary theorist) that we can locate Ozick's struggle for historicity. Ozick's denial of rupture, her emphasis on normative patterns of belief and behavior, her attempt to restore Jewish fiction to its Aggadic role, are all signs that her conception of the past has less to do with Jewish history and more to do with Jewish memory. When "the true image of the past flits by" for Ozick, it is the remembered past, the past of God's interventions and Israel's responses. Commenting on this traditional view of the past, Bloom pointedly notes that "Because the intervention is for *our* response, we can be tempted to believe we are everything; because the intervener is incommensurate with us, we can fear that we are nothing."[30] It is the latter possibility, the fear that we are nothing and that we have failed in our response, which moves Ozick so strongly in her recent work.

Joseph Brill yearns to respond appropriately to what he perceives to be divine intervention in his life at least as strongly as does Edelshtein or Puttermesser, but Ozick treats him with less sympathy, and his recognition of limitation and failure is ultimately more painful and more profound. The protagonist of *The Cannibal Galaxy,* having escaped from the Nazis as a young man, emigrates from his native France to "the middle of an ashen America,"[31] founding a school based on a "Dual Curriculum" of his own devising:

> a school run according to the principle of twin nobilities, twin antiquities. The fusion of scholarly Europe and burnished Jerusalem. The grace of Madame de Sévigné's flowery courtyard mated to the perfect serenity of a purified Sabbath. Corneille and Racine set beside Jonah and Koheleth. The combinations wheeled in his brain.[32]

This passage and the context in which it appears (the young Brill is hiding in the cellar of a convent when he is struck by pedagogical inspiration) take us to the center of Ozick's historical and cultural obsessions. To what extent is Jewish culture compatible with "Western Civilization"? Brill admires both Rabbi Akiva and Madame de Sévigné; his lifelong attempt to unite them, and find, moreover, a brilliant student in whom such a union might flourish, is an indication of his idealism but perhaps his folly as well. As Sanford Pinsker observes, one interpretation of the image of the cannibal galaxy is that it represents "the clash of cultures, Western and Jewish"; thus the novel "is a study in assimilation's multiple personalities and changing faces."[33] For Ozick, assimilation is not the wonderful synthesis of the misguided Brill's Dual Curriculum, or for that matter, what Yerushalmi calls "the creative assimilation of initially foreign influences [that] has often fructified the Jewish people."[34] No, for Ozick, assimilation is the cannibalization of Judaism: as a historical entity, Judaism can barely survive in the devouring maw of Western Civilization. The fact that Ozick conducts this study in a primary school indicates how far she has come from Edelshtein's manic but still sentimental comedy of isolated old age. Brill, the émigré from Old World Jewish culture, is forced to confront the culturally impoverished mediocrity of contemporary Jewish-American life. His treasured ideal of a rich, rational education drawing on the best of both worlds is thoroughly deflated by generations of monotonous American children, their equally dull parents, and their uninspired teachers.

It is no accident that throughout the novel, Brill, once the assiduous student of Talmud and astronomy, nods off in front of the TV.

The cannibalization of Brill's dream is apparently allayed by the entrance into his life of the brilliant philosopher Hester Lilt and her daughter Beulah. In a sense, Hester is the successful embodiment of the synthesis which Brill hopes to achieve with his students. The author of such books as *Metaphor as Exegesis* and *Interpretation as an End in Itself,* she cites midrash and Mozart in her lectures—and sharply criticizes Brill's surrender, his failure to take up his own intellectual and pedagogical challenges, especially the challenge of teaching her mediocre daughter. Brill on the other hand sees Hester's philosophy as a set of elaborate strategies justifying Beulah's total lack of inspiration; in Ozick's kabbalistic metaphor, "The flawed daughter, shining, crowned, barefoot, inside the veil of the mother's madness."[35] At issue in this debate is much more than the psychology of teachers and parents. Brill renounces his passionate dedication to his youthful synthesis of cultural values; in marrying and fathering a child late in life, he gives in to his desire merely to perpetuate himself and live a "normal" existence. Hester sacrifices neither the extraordinary life of the mind nor the ordinary world of the devoted parent. Brill's son Naphtali ends up as a business major; Beulah, of course, emerges from her cocoon as a brilliant, acclaimed artist. In the novel's last sentence, we read that "She labored without brooding in calculated and enameled forms out of which a flaming nimbus sometimes spread."[36] This nimbus corresponds to what Ozick calls "the redemptive corona," "interpretation, implicitness, the nimbus of *meaning* that envelopes story."[37] To an even greater extent than her mother's philosophy, Beulah's paintings miraculously bring together Jewish and Western cultures: products of a liturgical imagination, they are graven images that bear interpretation, and as such impose themselves powerfully upon the memory. As Benjamin would say, they are approaches to the Messianic Kingdom through the world of the profane.

Joseph Brill, however, has failed to recognize this, even as he has failed to respond properly to the intervention of Hester and Beulah into the otherwise fatal progress of his life. Sadly misguided (and for Ozick, I think, typical of even the most brilliant of modern Jews), he regards Beulah's paintings as "The purity of babble inconceivable in the vale of interpretation," but then tries vainly to interpret them. As he stares thoughtfully at the paintings, he is at the brink of the abyss into which Ozick and her reader plunge in the more audacious

Messiah of Stockholm. For in this most recent work, Ozick goes beyond the question of education to interrogate the primal Jewish object in matters of memory and history, covenant and redemption: the Book.

From her study of Scholem, Ozick knows that there is a long tradition of kabbalistic speculation regarding the nature of the Torah in the messianic age. This tradition informs her reading of the heretical scriptures of Bruno Schulz, leading her in turn to speculate upon the nature of Schulz's lost novel, appropriately called *The Messiah.* Ozick knows that Schulz's work is profoundly at odds with normative Judaism; the epigraph of *The Messiah of Stockholm* comes from the passage in *The Street of Crocodiles* in which Jacob, the demiurgic father of Schulz's alter-ego narrator, describes "an infinity of heretical and criminal methods" of creation. For Schulz, the most sublime of these methods is fiction, that profane secondary means of creation always in competition with the natural world created by God. But Ozick and her protagonist Lars Andemening, who believes he is Schulz's son, productively misread Schulz, treating him not as a heretical and profane writer but as prophet, a visionary who sees through the apparently dead matter of history to catch a redemptive glimpse of the messianic current swirling through even the most remote and moribund corners of provincial life. This is why *The Messiah of Stockholm* is so masterfully riddled with unresolved and ultimately self-destructive questions of identity: they reflect Ozick's ambivalence toward her own identity as a writer of fiction and thus toward the historicity of her art within the Jewish textual tradition. At best, fiction becomes a gnostic con game through which we can somehow gain access to revealed truth in history; at worst, it is a predatory forgery, the dead stuff of time imbued with preternatural life.

Lars comes to understand this in the climactic scene of the novel, when his friend the bookseller Heidi introduces him to her husband Dr. Eklund, whose existence Lars has previously doubted. The shady Dr. Eklund has "rescued" the lost manuscript of *The Messiah,* as well as a woman named Adela (after the alluring housemaid of Schulz's tales) who is supposedly Schulz's illegitimate daughter— though Eklund has probably forged the manuscript and fathered Adela himself. In Ozick's invented version of Schulz's novel, the messiah is a weirdly organic, palpitating, booklike thing which moves by means of "winglike sails." These sails—pages, actually—are covered with an alphabet of images made up of all the idols that have overrun Drohobycz, Schulz's provincial Polish hometown, which provides the setting for all of his stories. This bizarre contraption thus is designed as if it were an apocalyptic proof of Benjamin's belief that the profane is a counterforce which produces the messianic. When the messiah collapses in upon itself at the end of Ozick's wild midrash, it gives birth to a bird, a symbol of hope and regeneration. But Lars cannot stand such a resolution: justly suspecting a forgery, the tortured book reviewer sets fire to the manuscript, angrily accusing the Eklunds that "You want to be in competition with God."[38] Of course, so did his purported father.

Nevertheless, *The Messiah,* mad synthesis of the sacred and the heretical, does not survive to enter literary history. Only Lars's own story remains, the story of an orphan sadly "cured" of his delusions of paternity, moving from the role of inspired, ignored critic to that of mediocre, successful journalist. As in the case of Joseph Brill (but with even greater pathos, since Lars is in every respect a more sublime figure), Ozick's most recent protagonist fails in his struggle for a "time without boundaries," that personal state of messianic temporality that is free of the implacable forces of historical limitation.

The Messiah of Stockholm takes us to the farthest reaches of Ozick's wildly contradictory imagination, an inevitably contradictory imagination given the historical, theological, and literary matrix from which it springs. Her engagement with Schulz and what he represents as a storyteller proves that Bloom is right when he argues that Ozick's strength as a writer comes from her trust in "the narrative tradition's power to both absorb and renew her."[39] What this means, however, is that as a self-consciously Jewish writer, her fiction will always incorporate formal and thematic elements which have the potential to undo what she understands to be the basic premises of her work. Ozick, no doubt, would credit whatever power she has as a storyteller to the degree to which she successfully joins "monotheism-imagining" to "story-imagining"—both of which are related to the historicity of Jewish culture only in the most oblique ways. In other words, Ozick has developed an "authorial ideology" (I borrow the term from Terry Eagleton) that is superbly capable of producing a powerful aesthetic response in numerous readers, many of whom share neither her religious beliefs nor her attitude toward the storytelling imagination.

Yerushalmi tells us that we must understand Jewish culture as the accumulative product of a series of historical ruptures, a truth which Ozick confirms in a narrative art consciously designed to resist if not deny such breaks as strenuously as it can. Indeed, as he says in the passage I have used as the epigraph to this chapter, it is precisely the novel toward which modern Jews turn to provide "a new, metahistorical myth." Thus Ozick's notion of liturgical literature may itself prove to be a useful fiction, as well as another proof of Bloom's contention that in the world of the imagination there is no difference between sacred and secular texts. Fortunately, there is no need to resolve such antinomies. Perhaps we should even seek to preserve them if they are the source of Cynthia Ozick's splendid inspiration.

▲

CHAPTER 5

Lost and Found:
Hollander, Mandelbaum,
and the Poetry of Exile

The Book In Tatters

If it is true, as I have been arguing, that a theoretical understanding of
modern Jewish literature (I hesitate at this point to call it secular Jewish literature) comes into being when Walter Benjamin observes that
Aggadah no longer modestly lies at the feet of Halakah but instead
raises a mighty paw against it, then in what ways can this initial insight
be developed or refined? In Ozick's case, we have seen that her narrative genius lies precisely in her resistance to this historical rupture and
what might be called her divided loyalties, despite her vociferous
denials, between halakhic restraint and aggadic freedom. As the most
recent in a line of writers who have had to negotiate what I take to be
a given of modern Jewish culture, Ozick challenges us to rethink our
received critical assumptions, no matter how useful they may be.

Consider the aggadic nature of modern Jewish literature. In
raising its mighty paw, is such writing anything more than another
participant in the traditional interpretive process of midrash? Characterized by elaborate verbal play,

> Midrash—the act and process of interpretation—works in
> both the halakhic and agggadic realms.... Curiously, both
> halakhic and aggadic sorts of Midrash develop out of the
> same set of forces. Primarily we can see the central presence

79

of cultural or religious tension and discontinuity. Where there are questions that demand answers, and where there are new cultural and intellectual pressures that must be addressed, Midrash comes into play as a way of resolving crisis and reaffirming continuity with the traditions of the past.[1]

Modern Jewish life is preeminently an experience of such cultural tension and discontinuity. Given the last hundred years of Jewish history, is it any wonder that Jewish writers, however imbued with a midrashic sense, can hardly resolve crisis and reaffirm tradition in their narratives and parables? Instead, the *act* of writing, the *attempt* at cultural transmission in itself, as Benjamin sees in Kafka, must usually suffice.

And it does suffice, at least among Jewish storytellers. The tale, however inconclusive, however resistant to closure, however estranged from the old ways, is spun out and embroidered so as to memorialize the event. Truth, wisdom or proper conduct in the traditional sense of these terms, is harder to ascertain than ever before. But in the midrashic recitation of the narrative in all its ambiguities, the storyteller compensates for historical loss and personal disruption. Gimpel the Fool, a paradigm of the modern Jew despite his life in the shtetl of Frampol, becomes just such a storyteller when he wanders out into the world. Gimpel, who by the end of his tale is as much a con man as a dupe, understands that the recounting of elaborate lies—fictions—must make due in place of metaphysical certainties. "No doubt the world is entirely an imaginary world, but it is only once removed from the true world."[2] With these words as their motto, writers of fiction take on unprecedented importance in modern Jewish culture.

This is not the case, however, for Jewish poets. Granted that in one sense, all literature is "fiction," we can still make important distinctions between prose narrative and verse in regard to matters of certainty and truth. The music of poetry requires linguistic certainty of a different order from that of prose. This is not to say that modern Jewish novelists do not seek for *le mot juste:* witness the verbal precision of Kafka (who admired Flaubert) and his descendants. But poets cannot rest content with the gradually unfolding ambiguities, the layered midrashic conundrums of modern Jewish prose rhythms. They long for a kind of positive assertion which, if it is to be found anywhere in the Jewish canon, is located in Halakah, which has always been there to guide Jews in their social attitudes and consequently shape their states of feeling. Modern Jewish poets suffer the absence

of halakhic certainty more acutely than their storytelling counterparts. It is easier to tell tales *of* loss than to compose psalms *to* loss: in
prose narrative, rhythms of event mediate and disseminate emotion,
but given the concentrated formal and generic demands of poetry,
this is simply not the case.

What is probably the greatest Jewish poetry of loss in our time,
that of Paul Celan, achieves its power only through massive linguistic
disruption, its integral lyric structure wrenched from within by psychohistorical forces that are virtually unspeakable. Celan's *Nieman-
drose,* which, as George Steiner observes, "flowers *against* its
Maker,"[3] is for obvious reasons outside the compass of Jewish-American poetic experience. The loss of halakhic certainty is felt acutely
among Jewish-American poets, but the results are bound to be different: they are operating under what could be called normal conditions of diaspora, rather than those imposed upon Celan, who is
compelled to face and accuse the Source of meaning directly:

> Your
> being beyond in the night.
> With words I fetched you back, there you are,
> all is true and a waiting
> for truth.[4]

Jewish-American poets do not and perhaps need not seek for such a
confrontation. But because they too are aware, in the words of John
Hollander, that "the Book of the People of the Book is in tatters,"[5]
they embark on a different quest, seeking for other compensation.
Theirs is a quest for symbolic substitutions for the Law that has gone
beyond their grasp.

"The great narratives are of finding and of founding," Hollander
declares. "What was hidden in our case had already been found, what
was to be established has been long since. Our romance is of raising
and bearing, the undoing of histories" (23). Both Hollander's *Spectral Emanations* and Allen Mandelbaum's *Chelmaxioms* are ambitious
poems which attempt to raise up and bear aloft elaborate symbols
derived from Jewish lore but altered, reinterpreted, in order to compensate for profound historical and spiritual loss. Such reinterpreta-
tion involves "the undoing of histories" because the tales, rituals, and
wisdom which stem from the Law must all be revealed as inadequate,
cast into doubt, when the Law itself is perceived to have withdrawn
from the arena of human experience. But unlike midrashic reinterpre-

tation of Scripture, the new poem will not restore faith in the old ways: "I would gaze at the ruins and contemplate not reconstruction, not restoration, but restitution. What we were planning, what was being planned for us, was a serious trifling with history" (Hollander 25). A thief makes restitution when he returns stolen goods to their rightful owner. Because the Text has stolen itself away, a new Text must be provided. But whether such restitution can ever satisfy the questing—or exiled—poet always remains in doubt:

> It is as if one lived by a Scripture whose original tongue had been totally forgotten, all other texts in it lost or defaced, and that had only been preserved in a mocking and contemptuous translation, elegantly but insincerely done. And yet it would have had to have done for one's Text. (Hollander 22)

As Harold Bloom says of the Jewish writer in his mournful essay "The Sorrows of American-Jewish Poetry," "Whatever else is possible for him, it is hardly given to him that he may forge the uncreated unconscience of his people, the people of the Book and of the *halakhah*."[6] Following Bloom, it could be argued therefore that a successful Jewish poet will not only find strength in belatedness, but will celebrate what is understood to be an inadequate substitution for the lost or decayed original. The subtitle of *Spectral Emanations* is "A Poem in Seven Branches in Lieu of a Lamp," referring to the Menorah supposedly taken from the Second Temple, and all that it symbolizes, including the Torah.[7] Similarly, Mandelbaum's *Chelmaxioms,* "the Maxims Axioms Maxioms of Chelm," is put forward in the book's Preface as a potential addition to the Talmud: "Indeed, if the Talmud already has two redactions—Jerusalem's and Babylon's—why not, the maxioms ask, a third?"[8] The lost town of Chelm, supposedly destroyed in World War II and rediscovered in Mandelbaum's text, is both "the Diaspora writ large" and "the Diaspora writ small" (xv). Thus in the poems of Mandelbaum and Hollander, we encounter a strange but crucial blending of inventive pride and melancholy humility.

This tonal ambiguity, derived from the poets' self-consciousness of their historical and cultural position, relates in turn to the structure of the poems, their versification, and their rhetoric. In the Preface of *Chelmaxioms,* the Hoarse Savant (the poet's rather pedantic persona) reminds us that the poem's penchant for elaborate structural devices looks back to "the divagations, digressions, the discreet

and indiscreet parentheses native to talmudic/midrashic exegesis."
But this noble scriptural ancestry also produces

> the absurdity inherent in analogical and numerological
> revery—eleven tribes, eleven quays, six findings, five gates,
> five cesurasongs, two tutelary birds, two tutelary shapes....
> The absurdity inherent in too tenacious lust for the Abso-
> lute. (xvi)

The structure of *Spectral Emanations* is imbued with the same such
"absurdity": Hollander's Notes to the poem revel in numerological
details of the verse and astronomical analogies to the various colors
of the spectrum which divide the work into its seven sections. Such
an obsession with order in these late Jewish poems of substitution is
a sign of their authors' uncertainty: can the new Text, however much
a product of midrashic divagations, of the making and unmaking of
verbal form, truly compensate for that which has been lost? Perhaps
this is what Bloom means when he says of *Spectral Emanations* that
"Scheme, in a sense, is part of the poem's undoing."[9]

This doubt, this internalized threat of undoing, also accounts for
the versification of both poems. Given the range of verse forms and
metrical possibilities available to contemporary poets, Mandelbaum
and Hollander usually would be considered "formalists," "traditionalists," or "academic poets." These terms carry all sorts of ideological
baggage with them and are often applied with insufficient refinement.
Still, we can safely assert that both poets are devoted to regular meters
and rhyme, and are acutely aware of their problems and possibilities,
as seen not only in their poetry, but in Hollander's criticism and his
handbook of forms (*Rhyme's Reason*), and in Mandelbaum's extraordinary translations. It is also safe to say that generally, formal poetry,
especially in comparison with free verse, is associated with an overt
sense of aesthetic order and a relative fixity of intent and will on the
part of the writer. How have these formal concerns manifested themselves in Hollander's and Mandelbaum's major Jewish works?

The lines of *Spectral Emanations* make use of complex syllable
counts and stanza divisions, while *Chelmaxioms* is variously rhymed
throughout. Yet the verse in these texts depends upon frameworks of
prose. Hollander notes that in his substitute menorah, "Below each
cup of color [the verse] is a branch of prose, fulfilling and supporting
it" (3). As for *Chelmaxioms,* though readers could conceivably move
through its one hundred forty pages of rhyme without a break, they

must first read the three crucial pages of the Preface, and are often moved to consult the thirty pages of notes or "Scoriae from *The Vast & Versal Lexicon*" which follow and purport to explain the dozens of obscure words and arcane references which appear in the body of the text. In short, Hollander and Mandelbaum feel obliged to provide commentaries to their new Scriptures. The sense of achieved form remains problematic; the enactment of triumphant will that one often associates today with successful poetry in rhyme and meter is ridden with doubt. The dialectic of verse and prose upon which the poems' trajectories depend also reminds us of the central absence around which the poems are built.

However, not only structure and prosody, but rhetoric too, the texts' quality of language or mode of discourse, signifies the poems' awareness of lack, their self-consciousness of loss. *Spectral Emanations* and *Chelmaxioms* are scholarly poems; their authors are, as Wallace Stevens (who stands behind them) says, "dark rabbi[s]" who observe "the nature of mankind, / In lordly study."[10] But as we have seen, they are insecure in such a role, which may account not only for their stupendous poetic erudition (Mandelbaum's "talk of talk and talk of text" [xvi]), but their nervously joking attitude toward such scholarly discourse as well.

Here the specifically Jewish problem of the withdrawal of halakhic certainty coincides with a general problem of modern poetry, that of accessibility. Certain types of modern poetry (*The Waste Land,* replete with notes, is our *locus classicus*) are often called "difficult," "obscure," even "hermetic." Their language—esoteric, allusive, insistently private—presents even the well-schooled reader with both an invitation and a rebuff, and the result is often great frustration on the reader's part. Reception theory has demonstrated that over the course of time, readers become naturalized to the problems presented by new and difficult works, learn to negotiate their baffling techniques, and in doing so, expand their arsenal of reading strategies while at the same time domesticating, perhaps even canonizing previously recondite and resistant texts.[11] While this optimistic paradigm certainly could apply to the poems under discussion here, which, like all serious literature, also must suffer the general decline of literacy in what George Steiner calls our "post-culture," we are still faced with nagging questions.

Given the erudite discourse and "bookish" nature of what are already specifically Jewish poems, who, even among the small potential audience of educated Jewish-Americans, will read such rarefied texts? Can we be satisfied with a mandarin Jewish poetry, which, for all its sublime gestures and honorable aggadic heritage, still reduces to a coyly playful antiquarianism? If the poets themselves understand their work as a more or less inadequate substitution, can we see them as any more than quixotic rhymsters, Hollander's joking "Pancho Manza, *homme/De terre*" (30)? Not even the usual response, that poetry has always been, finally, an elite genre, can really provide solace at this late date.

In *Chelmaxioms,* Mandelbaum writes:

> It's not that he forgets. But the endured
> is more than can be rendered.
>
> How they crack:
> the word and the appeasing act.
>
> But even as they shatter,
> he gathers fragmentary matter. (119)

This lyric, called "Second Song of Scavenging," goes some way toward an answer to our questions. If traditional Jewish writing has passed its wisdom down in any degree to its contemporary secular descendents, such wisdom is to be found in lines like these. Diasporic Jewish experience is almost incommensurable with the act of writing, but however little the word can render what is endured, it is only the word which grants that endurance. The inadequacy of language always confronts the Jewish writer, for it is only God's word (and in the Kabbalah, not even God's word) which can bring about and sustain creation to any extent. But the breaking of the vessels, that great metaphor to which Scholem and Bloom have given us access, signifies both disaster and new hope. Word and act are no longer one, the myth tells us, but in the ruins of the fallen language-world, those who are faithful to the original power of verbal creativity may gather the fragments again.

The ambivalence of Mandelbaum's and Hollander's poems are thus matters of audacity and devotion. Their writing is a bold substitute for the Law and a dutiful attempt to restore lost mythic wholeness. The excavation of Chelm and the poem that took the place of a menorah may be irreverent but they are not irreligious. These are works by good-natured versions of "the pious atheist," Scholem's term for Kafka, "for whom nothing has remained of God but the void—in Kafka's sense, to be sure, the void of God."[12]

The Echt *Chelm*

According to Irving Howe and Eliezer Greenberg, as Jewish folktales of Chelm grew, this town of simpletons "became a kind of mirror-in-reverse of the Yiddish world: all the strains of a highly intellectualistic culture were relaxed in these tales of incredible foolishness and innocence."[13] Mandelbaum's Hoarse Savant dismisses this tradition as "the counterfeit, usurping Chelm of Yiddish folklore...so derivative of—so indebted for its humor to—early German lumpen humor." Nevertheless, as we have seen, "like the false Chelm, the echt Chelm also has its undertow of absurdity" (xvi), due to the hypertrophied textuality of diasporic Jewry. The *echt* Chelm is the wandering "place" of Jewish linguistic lore, and is as much an attitude toward discourse as a canon or bound body of specific works. Carried to an extreme and, as in *Chelmaxioms,* transformed into an absurdly complex, fanciful, arbitrary system of symbols, this crucial attitude—this masterful cultural strategy—threatens to become a pedantic, encyclopedic joke. If *Chelmaxioms* does not take itself altogether seriously, it is because, despite the disclaimer of the Hoarse Savant, the poem is aware that in drawing upon the Chelm myth, it presents a reverse mirror-view of the Diaspora's essential intellectualism.

"Exile gave Chelm to light" (7) proclaims the poet. As a comic instance of what George Steiner calls "the homeland of the text," Chelm appears to the reader/archaeologist through sifting levels of discourse. In a section of the poem invoking Schliemann and the search for Troy, the men of Chelm do some excavating of their own:

> We dug from Chelm above
> and found more Chelm below
> as far as psalms can go
> and only can conjecture
> that even at the center
> our findings would not alter...(60)

Since Chelm is made out of language, we can only conjecture that the further one digs, the more language one will find. The poem, which is itself a thing of words, is an instrument for uncovering more words: we go "as far as psalms can go." Actually, there is no real point in guessing about Chelm's "center"; as deconstructionists (who would feel very much at home in Chelm) never tire of pointing out, language has no center. Such is the hope—and the despair—of commentary.

Unlike a geopolitical homeland, a textual homeland, a place in exile made from commentary, cannot be occupied from without. Neither can belief-structures calcify and grow dogmatic within. As Steiner argues,

> Locked materially in a material homeland, the text may, in fact, lose its life-force, and its truth-values may be betrayed. But when the text *is* the homeland, when it is rooted only in the exact remembrance and seeking of a handful of wanderers, nomads of the word, it cannot be extinguished.[14]

Devotion to the Word and its perpetually unfolding commentaries has long been recognized as a key to the survival of Jewish culture. Mandelbaum understands this, of course, but also understands the corrosive power of exilic time:

> He then would say:
> Diaspora
> is still the way
> of shreds and shards,
> of all that frays,
> discolored words,
> and leaves astray,
> and winds that scatter
> nesting birds—
>
> and we cannot remember
> the order
> of the sayings of the fathers. (15)

Possessed of the "hallucinatory techniques and disciplines of attention to the text"[15] as well as the ineluctable sense of linguistic decay, Mandelbaum's Chelmites endlessly suffer the ecstatic futility of commentary. As is written in "The Lied of Long Since,"

> (he followed a discolored scroll
> that mapped the forest in a scrawl
> as labyrinthine as the soul
> that wanders endless texts
> that it may be made whole) (108)

Just as the Jewish soul in exile will never find rest, so too its text will never be made whole. But Chelmites—and here their foolishness is indeed debatable—seem not to mind, for they are used to minor verbal miracles: "The men of Chelm do not despair: / they lift their lances in the air / and leave them there" (11).

In their textual exile, the men of Chelm can also take solace in a greater miracle: the appearance among them of the Perfect Woman. The singular muse of *Chelmaxioms,* the Perfect Woman is also a lovely foil to the men of Chelm, who, divided into eleven pedantic tribes (spinozists, kabalists, metamorphosists, ecclesiastesists, etc.), spend their time in endless dispute. Intellectually equal to the men (one important section of the poem is devoted to her reading of a page of Kant), but infinitely more graceful, she is Mandelbaum's figure of the Shekhinah, the kabbalistic emanation of divinity known as the "Bride of God," about whom numerous myths, traditions, and rituals have developed.[16] Associated with Israel in its condition of exile, the Shekhinah is also the Sabbath Queen, for on the Sabbath God and Israel are united, providing a foretaste of messianic redemption and cosmic union. One of the most beautiful lyrics in *Chelmaxioms* celebrates her coming to Chelm:

> A port beyond our portulans,
> a bay too brilliant for man,
> where light alone can dwell:
> from that elusive harbor
> the Sabbath Queen sets sail
>
> and reaches us—always as dusk
> would touch the patient foothills—
> some three days after she began
> her journey out of speechlessness,
> her pilgrimage to Chelm. (43)

In Mandelbaum's version of the myth, the Sabbath Queen sails from a realm of divine "speechlessness" to Chelm, the all-too-human town of endless verbiage. This speechlessness, however, is not to be understood as silence. Just as the divine point of origin is a light "too brilliant for man," it is also an absolute word, incomprehensible to us in our fallen human state. As Gershom Scholem observes:

> This absolute word is originally communicated in its limitless fullness, but...this communication is incomprehensible! It is

not a communication which provides comprehension; being
basically nothing but the expression of essence, it becomes a
comprehensible communication only when it is mediated.[17]

It is through such mediation, the endless process of commentary,
that the men of Chelm feel closest to the divine, but also grow most
weary of study and argument. Thus the weekly journey of the Sabbath Queen produces "the anxiousness, / the everlasting labor, / the
mourning her departure, / the six days waiting for her" (44).

This anxiousness, of course, is both intellectual and erotic,
given the alluring beauty of the Shekhinah and the severe devotion
to study of the patriarchs of Chelm. Later in the poem, in "The Lied
of Long Since," the scholar wandering in the textual forest outside
the walls of Chelm comes upon the Perfect Woman:

> and when he heard her voice that used
> the parts of speech as plants have used
> the water and the air,
> converting them—dull elements
> and colorless—to living fare,
>
> he veered about and south with her—
> let distraught Delirium
> await some other son of Chelm
> to share oblique soliloquies
> along woodways and cryptic leagues. (109)

"Because she is mute," says Walter Benjamin, "nature mourns." The
Perfect Woman returns language to a kind of natural grace, the
prelapsarian condition of the Divine speaking through nature. Offering erotic freedom and linguistic ease unknown to the sons of
Chelm, she lures them away from their delirious pedantry. In "The
Lied of Yet" she is seen offering comfort to scholars throughout the
town, "but she is wan / within the alleyways of Chelm." "She needs
a hearth to keep her warm / but not a charnel house" (124), and so
she departs, leaving only memories and, in one of the "Aftersongs,"
the scholars' vain search for her name.

Are we to believe then that Chelm is world of dead language,
and the textual devotion of the Diaspora nothing but vanity? Does
obsession with the word lose us the world? In *Chelmaxioms*, this is
itself the subject of dispute. With the loss of the Perfect Woman still
in mind, here is one side of the argument:

> ...To define
> defiles the dress, the nakedness,
> the black surtout, the gold soutache,
> the gaze of eye, the gaze of flesh,
> the patient passacaglia and
> the calculating saraband,
>
> the turbulence, the calm caress,
> the thraws and throes, the helplessness
> of man and woman, breast on breast...(143–44)

And here, despite such loss, is the other:

> Do not defend the ways of men
> to God and not the ways of God
> to men for each of them has turned
> aside and each has found it hard
> to listen when the other was
> the one who was in question and
> for each the one atonement is
>   begin again. (87)

An Object Which is Somehow Like a Text

But what does it mean to begin again? However one longs for atonement, making whole that which was rent, repairing the botched job, the task involves an investment in psychic energy which can prove unbearably daunting. In the past there was a basic failure of attention: according to Mandelbaum, God and man turned aside from each other, did not listen to each other and went their separate ways. As in the Kabbalah, creation could not be sustained; the vessels broke, the light spilled over and all was scattered. The lamp was lost, the community went into exile, the poem could not achieve resolution.

Beginning again, therefore, does not mean starting from nothing. It means searching and gathering in a landscape littered with ruins, painful reminders of past inadequacies and failures. What is called for is a kind of spiritual demolition, in which the past is remembered, revised and cleared away. The new poem must do all this at once. And as both the site of this activity and the activity itself, the poem must be experienced as a place through which one moves and a time in which creation is enacted. The result, as Bloom says of psychoanalysis, is "another parable of a people always homeless or at least uneasy in space, who must seek a perpetually deferred fulfillment in time."[18]

There is a prose passage in *Spectral Emanations* in which these ideas are embodied in an odd but revealing way. A voice both comic and frighteningly portentous instructs the questing poet (or is it the poet who instructs his readers?) in the building of a sort of infernal machine, for "when bought already assembled, these things work very badly, and may leave dangerous residues" (33). Dissatisfied with what has been "already assembled," the text / machine builds itself, an assembly in time and space which finally presents itself as a parable of the state of contemporary literary creation. We are told that "There can be great variation in the exterior design.... But it is the circuits alone which are terrifying, and the interior spaces where tolerances are so minute" (33). As is always the case with parabolic writing, we must pay heed to the interiority of the text; the parable insists upon its exacting, meaningful depths, however variously it may present its exterior. Furthermore, the writing (or reading) of such a work puts us at psychic risk: "The energy it consumes is enormous; it is almost too expensive to operate. But of course, one must" (34).

As Hollander and Bloom understand, writing of this sort is a ritualized struggle with the past, an acknowledgment of an original failure (Bloom's "catastrophe creation") which still has great power over the present. Thus we are warned that "After the red light goes off, there will be a period of waiting; do not disintegrate them at this stage, or you too will never have existed." Nevertheless, as the passage concludes, "If you get it to work properly, it will put an end to them, your predecessors" (34). Presumably, the successful writing of the present rectifies the past. The predecessors are laid to rest in a text that self-consciously realizes itself in time and space.

In the larger schema of *Spectral Emanations* (and in this sense, the text/machine is a parable within a parable), the task of putting an end to one's predecessors is equivalent to that of finding the lost menorah, making this a Bloomian (perhaps overly Bloomian) poem indeed. This leads in turn to a basic question: as a modern Jewish quest, what does the search for the lamp really signify? In the Prologue, "The Way to the Throne Room," the poet first appears among a company of questers who fail to reach "what we might read as the seat of vision in the *merkabah* or throne-chariot of Ezekial."[19] As the poet explains,

> On the way to the seventh chamber, the amethyst and
> sapphire light ceased and there were glimmering
> marble slabs. They dazzled mine eyes, and it was
> not at my own tears that I cried out *O water! Water!*
> Thus I was never to enter. (7)

The light from the marble slabs (perhaps the tables of the law) blinds him, and he is no longer able to make his way on what could be understood as a search for halakhic truth. He is unable to go (or see) beyond the bounds of the human spectrum, and the aggadic journey through the colors which constitutes the rest of the poem must compensate for the lost chance at halakhic certainty. The poet is launched immediately on this trip, for the tears that are not his own and the cry of "Water!" are those of the Israeli soldier whose death is depicted in "Red," which follows directly after. Thus the human scale of the search for the menorah, with its seven differently colored branches, substitutes for the pure light which no mortal eye could bear. Yet in the rainbow of the text, the promise of the original quest remains: as Hilda says in the passage from *The Marble Faun* which serves as Hollander's epigraph, "when all seven are kindled, this radiance shall combine into the white light of truth" (1).

So the wandering text of *Spectral Emanations,* the passage through the limited range of human vision, is awash in a succession of colored lights with flickering glimpses of a purer radiance: in Walter Benjamin's terms, the poem "is shot through with chips of Messianic time." In "Yellow," amidst Hollander's puns and scholarly games, the pathos of this situation is given voice,

> ...an interpretation
> Of the flimsy text, half unremembered,
> Dimming evermore and diminishing.
> Like gold afire in the yellow candles'
> Flame, steady with remembrances and now
> And then only wavering in regret,
> What might have been burns up and the bright fruit
> Of what we after all have ever ripens. (13–14)

Yet even as the poet recognizes these diminished circumstances, he also sees, in a beautiful representation of Benjamin's mystical *Jetztzeit,* the present as the "time of the now," how he will be compensated for his devotion to the aggadic quest:

To have been kept, to have reached this season,
Is to have eternized, for a moment,
The time when promise and fulfillment feed
Upon each other, when the living gold
Of sunlight struck from the amazing corn
Seems one with its cold, unending token,
The warm time when both seem reflections from
The bright eyes of the Queen of the Peaceful
Day being welcomed with these twin burnings,
These prophetic seeds of the Ripener,
Brightness rising and getting on with things. (14)

The Shekhinah as Sabbath Queen is strangely but movingly
conflated with the figure of a fertility goddess, a Demeter "Of sunlight struck from the amazing corn." We experience the timeless
peace of the sabbath, which in the kabbalah is understood as a foretaste of messianic redemption, while at the same time acknowledging
and taking pleasure in our temporality, "Brightness rising and getting
on with things." In the following stanza, the poet recognizes this
female figure to be his muse and his fictive creation as well; their
lovemaking presents the Shekhinah as mystical bride coming to the
initiate, as well as the pagan union of earth and sky:

The man of earth exhales a girl of air,
Of her light who lies beside him, gentle
And bare, under the living shawl of all
Her long hair, while her short below softly
Touches his tired thigh with welcoming.
It is that she is there. It is the pure
Return of everlastingness in her
Hands and the readiness of the sweet pear
In the touch of her mouth that fill the air
—Even the air within the circle of
His emptied arms—with light beyond seeming. (14–15)

In these lines, the Shekhinah is at once mistress of presence and
absence, immanence and transcendence. In giving herself to the poet
(as in *Chelmaxioms*), she rewards his persistence in the wandering ritual of writing, but in her disappearance from "the circle of / His
emptied arms" into "light beyond seeming," she maintains his condition of exile.

This encounter proves to be most instructive. In "Green," the next section of the poem and central among the seven colors of the spectrum, Hollander, beginning with a line from Goethe's *Color Theory,* expresses his understanding of the limits of his wandering, spectral text, which are the same limits as those of his temporal existence:

> *Man will nicht weiter, und man kann nicht weiter:* we
> Desire nothing beyond this being of green
> Nor can we reach it; and even that overworked
> Part of us, the eye, wearied of the vivid, stuffed
> With the beneficence of leaf, seeks not to raise
> Itself toward the new giddiness of heaven, clear
> Though that blue may be—it would be to leave too much
> Behind, the old heaviness of earth—but vaulting
> The whole sequence of empurplings to alight in
> Blackness, if anywhere else, in the condensed dust
> Of being seen as green, turning to which darkness
> Is no roving of vision, no dimming of trust. (18)

Blue, the heavenly color of the inaccessible Law, is rejected in favor of the earthy fullness of vegetative green, the ripeness of mortality's aggadic text. (As Hollander notes at the outset of the poem, "Only at the moment of green is there time for a story.") The blackness of death, when there is no longer any "roving of vision," is "the condensed dust / Of being seen as green," the fulfillment of organic existence, not the pure transcendence of blue, the "giddiness of heaven." This is confirmed at the end of "Blue": "Dawn comes when we distinguish blue from—white? / No, green—and, in agreement, eyeing the / Dying dark, our morning wariness nods" (33).

This interplay of dawn and dusk, immanence and transcendence, beginning and end of the spectrum, is reworked yet again in "Violet," the last section of the poem. Here too nature is close at hand, reminding us of mortality: we stand "in the pale tan of / The yet ungathered grain" (38) asking "in a / Mown oatfield what text will / The dallying night leave?" (39). The answer is provided by a number of tropes representing the menorah, now found through the completion of the poetic quest. In a beautiful expression of continued hope in continued exile, we see

> a last
> Candle that may be made

To outlast its waning
Wax, a frail flame shaking
In a simulacrum

Of respiration. Oh,
We shall carry it set
Down inside a pitcher

Out into the field, late
Wonderers errant in
Among the rich flowers.

Like a star reflected
In a cup of water
It will light up no path:

Neither will it go out. (38–39)

A single spark has been restored to a single vessel, though this one small, enduring candle may become

—A tree of light. A bush
Unconsumed by its fire.
Branches of flame given

Sevenfold tongue that there
Might be recompounded
Out of the smashed vessels

Of oil, of blood and stain,
Wine of grass and juice of
Violet, a final

White, here at the point of
Sky water and field all
Plunged in their own deep well

Of color whose bottom
Is all of the darkness. (39–40)

The promise of *tikkun* is unmistakable, for the smashed vessels will be recompounded and the white light of transcendence will shine forth against the well of darkness.

Even so, in the prose passage that closes the poem, such transcendence is finally recognized as unattainable even in death, for "morning will bring no light along the right-hand path on the margin of the dark." Instead, the poet has "his old man's dream of dawn that unrobes the violet, allows the early rose to take her morning dip": a dream of returning to spectral beginnings so that he can live through the mortal cycle again. As we are told,

> He remembers this, and thinks not to quest among the regions of black for what lies beyond violet,

> But would stay to hum his hymn of the hedges, where truth is one letter away from death, and will ever so be emended. (42)

Content with the cycle of the lesser quest, he remains an aggadic writer, following the rabbinic injunction to put a hedge around the truth of the Law. Hollander has learned the lesson of the golem legend, when the aleph in the word *emet* (truth) is removed to make the word *met* (death), returning the golem to lifelessness. To play with divine truth, even if it could be done, is to play with the danger of nothingness as well. It is best to remain in the world of emanations.

▲

CHAPTER 6

Judaism and
the Rhetoric of Authority:
George Steiner's Textual Homeland

In a perceptive if not modest moment, George Steiner describes himself as "some kind of courier carrying urgent letters and signals to
those few who might respond with interest and, in their turn, pass on
the challenging news." These words have a distinctively Kafkan echo.
Throughout the Diaspora (and for Steiner, all those who might
respond to his signals live in exile), the courier brings the Word, but
cannot guarantee that it will be deciphered. In Kafka's brief parable
of cosmic exile called "Couriers,"

> They were offered the choice between becoming kings or the
> couriers of kings. The way children would, they all wanted to
> be couriers. Therefore there are only couriers who hurry
> about the world, shouting to each other—since there are no
> kings—messages that have become meaningless. They would
> like to put an end to this miserable life of theirs but they dare
> not because of their oaths of service.[2]

In bringing this parable to bear upon Steiner's situation as a
modern Jewish writer and critic of culture, I do not mean to imply
that the messages this courier conveys have become meaningless. As
we have seen in our consideration of his contemporaries, when the
Kafkan sensibility reshapes a Jewish writer, transmission in itself
becomes a virtue, however much a gesture of futility it may be as well.

But I find this paragraph emblematic of Steiner's case because his work is informed throughout by the vexing possibility that there are no kings. Perhaps they never were; perhaps we have killed them; perhaps, to extend the kabbalistic metaphor, they have so totally withdrawn into themselves that they have disappeared. The centralizing power of cultural elites is broken. The possibility of religious transcendence is nil. Politics as a vital expression of communal life has ceased utterly. As Steiner continually reminds us, the commanders of the death camps listened seriously to Mozart, read deeply in Rilke.

Steiner has a number of terms for our present condition. We live in a "post-culture," suffering "the loss of a geographic-sociological centrality, the abandonment or extreme qualification of the axiom of human progress, our sense of the failure or severe inadequacies of knowledge and humanism in regard to social action."[3] We have endured "the retreat from the word," for "our awareness of the complication of reality is such that those unifications or syntheses of understanding which have made common speech possible no longer work."[4] Thus, ours is the time of the "after-Word," the epoch which follows upon a *"break of the covenant between word and world which constitutes one of the very few genuine revolutions of spirit in Western history and which defines modernity itself."*[5] In all of these formulations, we sense a mood which Steiner himself identifies: "Call it *Kulturpessimismus*—it is no accident that the idiom is German—or a new stoic realism."[6] But despite this cultural pessimism, emerging particularly from Steiner's thinking about Judaism, the Holocaust and the virtual collapse of the Central European traditions of humanism, he is also one of our most passionate and sympathetic defenders of those traditions. And yet he also knows that the traditions he defends bear within themselves the potential for their violent unmaking.

Steiner is a rare figure in the contemporary intellectual milieu. Born into that now nearly extinct world of the emancipated Central European Jewish bourgeoisie, immensely learned, a master of many languages, Steiner often presents the lineaments of "mandarin cultural conservatism." Writing about Theodor Adorno, one of Steiner's most important influences, Martin Jay describes this position:

> His visceral distaste for mass culture, unrelieved hostility towards bureaucratic domination, and untempered aversion to technological, instrumental reason were all earmarks of a consciousness formed in the wake of what has been called the decline of the German mandarins. So too was the deep

current of pessimism that informed his thinking, even as he insisted on the importance of maintaining utopian hopes.[7]

This strikes me as a description that could just as well be applied to Steiner, but like Adorno, there is far more to Steiner than cultural conservatism:

> The reflexes of consciousness, the styles of articulacy which had generated messianic Marxism, Freudian psychoanalysis, the philosophies of discourse of Wittgenstein, the art of Mahler and of Kafka, were almost immediate to my childhood and upbringing. The polyglot habits of this background, the peregrine ironies and premonitions, the scarcely examined investment of familial energies and pride in the intellect and the arts, make up what I am.[8]

In other words, Steiner's personal and intellectual origins are to be found in the volatile cultural matrix of modernism, which, to an inordinate extent, was formed by assimilated European Jews. Within a relatively short span of time (from, say, the 1830s to the 1930s), a tradition of secular Jewish thought and expression came into being and flourished. Intimately bound up with and at times nearly indistinguishable from the mainstream of Western culture, yet still acutely aware of its marginal and often endangered situation, this tradition transformed every aspect of European society. Whether these transformations were too much for Europe to bear is a question to which Steiner returns again and again: he is, after all, not merely the heir to this heritage, but as he says, "a kind of survivor." His own "peregrine ironies and premonitions," which have provoked so much controversy throughout his career, mark him as doubly an exile, for secular European Jewry felt its diasporic condition acutely, and Steiner has lost that doubt-ridden world too.

In thinking of Steiner's situation and the way he has presented himself over the course of his career, I am reminded of a passage from Walter Benjamin's "The Destructive Character":

> The destructive character stands in the front line of the traditionalists. Some pass things down to posterity, by making them untouchable and thus conserving them, others pass on situations, by making them practicable and thus liquidating them. The latter are called the destructive.

> The destructive character has the consciousness of histori-
> cal man, whose deepest emotion is an insuperable mistrust of
> the course of things and a readiness at all times to recognize
> that everything can go wrong. Therefore the destructive
> character is reliability itself.[9]

In Steiner, who readily acknowledges Benjamin's influence, there is
something of the destructive character's relation to tradition and to
history. Steiner stands on the front line of the traditionalists, for
unlike the true conservative, his attitude toward historical knowledge
is practicable; he may revere the past, but he uses it strategically. In
1931, Benjamin, as one of the most refined products of secular
European Jewry, writes with frightening precision of "a readiness at
all times to recognize that everything can go wrong." Steiner places
this readiness at the heart of his understanding of contemporary culture. Because everything can go wrong, tradition cannot merely be
conserved but must be deployed: "To be able to envisage possibilities
of self-destruction, yet press home the debate with the unknown, is
no mean thing."[10] In the spirit of Benjamin, Adorno, Lukács, and
Bloch, what appears in Steiner as a rear-guard action proves to be an
assault on the future, on the gates of heaven, launched, as Kafka
dreamed, from below. Meanwhile, we are told, "Dreams must be disciplined to cover the ground of the possible."[11]

Steiner's rhetoric of cultural authority, the voice of the disciplined master who seeks in turn to discipline his readers ("To Civilize
our Gentlemen," as the title of an early essay quaintly puts it),
emerges from this usually covert utopian or messianic perspective,
which in turn has been influenced by earlier modes of Jewish
thought. Like Harold Bloom, Steiner conceives of cultural activity as
essentially "text-centered"; as he implies in many of his essays, the
Jewish devotion to the text can serve as a model for all readers and
writers struggling to continue their work under adverse historical
conditions. Thus, given the changes in Western culture, especially
since World War II, all those who still devote themselves to literature
can be regarded, at least metaphorically, as "Jews." Furthermore,
Steiner's insistence that all art depends upon a spiritual dimension, a
"wager on transcendence," productively blurs the line between the
secular and the religious, leading us back to crucial questions of
belief and artistic creation. As in the case of Cynthia Ozick, Steiner's
attempts to come to terms with such questions account for his own
style in both his criticism and his fiction. It is Steiner's engagement

with these and other matters of Jewish textuality and Jewish history, in relation to what he has to offer us regarding the general contours of Western culture, that remains to be explored.

As we have observed, Steiner's strategic understanding of Judaism depends upon two interrelated concepts: exile and textuality. Of course, these concepts in themselves are basic to any understanding of Judaism, but their appropriation and refinement in Steiner's work renew them, for they become keener intellectual categories and more urgent existential modalities. Steiner rarely speaks of them separately. A passage from *Real Presences,* his most recent book, is typical:

> Hermeneutic unendingness and survival in exile are, I believe, kindred. The text of the Torah, of the biblical canon, and the concentric spheres of texts about these texts, replace the destroyed Temple. The dialectical movement is profound. On the one hand, there is a sense in which all commentary is itself an act of exile. All exegesis and gloss transports the text into some measure of distance and banishment. Veiled in analysis and metamorphic exposition, the *Ur*-text is no longer immediate to its native ground. On the other hand, the commentary underwrites—a key idiom—the continued authority and survival of the primary discourse. It liberates the life of meaning from that of historical-geographical contingency. In dispersion, the text is homeland.[12]

Following Scholem, Steiner recognizes that commentary is a matter of both interpretive freedom and authoritative restraint, and he is at least as ambivalent about this state of affairs as his precursor. Commentary distances or banishes the primary text, but assures or "underwrites" its authority. Hermeneutic motion involves risk and loss, but the original word will not endure without it; only by wandering away from the text can we insure its survival. Textual exile recapitulates historical exile, even as the former is largely a result of the latter. But in a certain sense, the exilic state of commentary also guarantees the continuance of historical exile, since devotion to the text reinforces "bookishness" and opposes the blandishments of "historical-geographical contingency." In Steiner's vision of Judaism (which is, needless to say, that of an intellectual elite or "clerisy"), "active reading, answerability to the text on both the meditative-interpretive and the behavioural levels, is the central motion of personal and national homecoming."[13]

This view of Jewish intellectual life as a clerisy fostered by the conditions of exile cannot be fully comprehended except in contrast to nationalism, which Steiner bluntly calls "the venom of our age."[14] The Jews in diaspora, bound not to a nation-state which has its meaning in space but to textual processes unfolding over time, give the lie "to the vulgar mystique of the flag and the anthem, to the sleep of reason which proclaims 'my country right or wrong.'"[15] Devotion to the book rather than the state, the outward manifestation of which is the "rootless cosmopolitanism" of the Jews in exile, proves intolerable to patriotic demagoguery: the result has always been anti-Semitism.[16] Thus Steiner is deeply suspicious of any form of political or cultural populism, which too often leads to vulgarity and barbarism; he unabashedly prefers an elitism of mind and soul though not of social class per se. Turning the tables on his critics, he declares that "the real 'snob' seems to me the one who would deny his own vocation of almost autistic clerisy, of infection with thought, in order to harvest at the same time the rewards of popularity and democratic good-fellowship."[17]

Popularity and democratic good-fellowship are the seemingly benign American equivalents to the virulence of the European forms of nationalism which Steiner also condemns. But regardless of its type, nationalism undermines the critical self-absorption, the "autism" of the cleric, who in turn "is, by definition, a conscientious objector."[18] This model makes a good deal of sense when applied to Jewry in exile among the Gentile nations: traditional rabbinic Judaism and emancipated Jewish humanism are both text-centered, drawing the individual inward while at the same time fostering a critical attitude toward belief-systems which stand outside the faith in the book. Ghettos of the intellect, like ghettos in communities, are built from without and within. But when Jews seek to replace the scribal autism of diaspora with a geopolitical homeland of their own, the result, however predicated upon a textual tradition of exile and return, is yet another nationalism.

Steiner's response to Zionism is forthright but troubling. The true Zion must remain the homeland of the text:

> For the cleric, for the ideal of clerisy in Jewishness, this house of the future tense need not be Israel. Or rather, it is an 'Israel' of truth-seeking. Each seeking out of a moral, philosophic, positive verity, each text rightly established and expounded, is an *aliyah*, a homecoming of Judaism to itself and to its keeping of the books.[19]

Steiner's insistence upon a textual rather than a geopolitical home, in which *aliyah* means going to the book rather than going to the land, is at the heart of his attempt to preserve what could be called a "third way" in modern Judaism, one which remains true to his tradition of critical humanism. This third way is fraught with uncertainty and ambivalence, for it is predicated upon clerical "truth-seeking" rather than upon accepted truths. On the one hand, secular Zionism, which Steiner rightly connects to other nineteenth-century European nationalist movements, requires unswerving patriotic devotion; the result is Israel's disastrous political situation, for not only is it "armed to the teeth" but it is "compelled to make other men homeless, servile, disinherited, in order to survive from day to day."[20] On the other hand, the Orthodox position, requiring strict halakhic observance and the hope of a messianic return, likewise proves unacceptable to the modern, skeptical Jewish intellectual.

Steiner is somewhat more sympathetic to the Orthodox position than to secular Zionism, but like so many Jews today, he feels that he has "no part in the beliefs and ritual practices which underwrite it."[21] What he preserves from the Orthodox stance is that which so powerfully shaped the thinking of his most important precursors: messianism. Surely the most volatile element of modern Jewish thought, messianism, as Anson Rabinbach explains,

> demands a complete repudiation of the world as it is, placing its hope in a future whose realization can only be brought about by the destruction of the old order. Apocalyptic, catastrophic, utopian and pessimistic, Messianism captured a generation of Jewish intellectuals before the First World War. The Messianic impulse appears in many forms in the Jewish generation of 1914...secular *and* theological, as a tradition that stands opposed to both secular rationalism and what has been called "normative Judaism."[22]

Despite his claim that he is most drawn to "the Nietzschean gaiety in the face of the inhuman,"[23] it seems to me that book for book, essay for essay, Steiner is given to *Kulturpessimismus* to a much greater degree—and that this dark brooding stems from a messianic desire, usually held back, to "press for the end." To be sure, Steiner is no full-fledged apocalyptic messianist—he is too much the representative of Central European humanism—but like the conservative Talmudist drawn to the theurgy of Kabbalah, Steiner is lured again and again to the edge of the abyss. As we have noted, this psychocultural volatility, this attraction to nihilism and apocalyptic violence, are constituent parts of the tradition in which Steiner locates himself. They are preeminent modernist qualities, but they enter the modernist matrix partly through Jewish messianic channels.

These tendencies are compounded by the brute fact of the Holocaust, and Steiner's special sense not of mere guilt (as is the case for American Jewry) but also of an uncanny near miss, since he was born and brought up in France and did not reach the United States until 1940. Having thus been saved, this brilliant heir of secular European Judaism would naturally be attracted to a mode of thought "which did not see history as the progressive unfolding of the rational, which was attuned to the poverty of experience which the Enlightenment left in its wake, and which accepted the possibility of apocalypse."[24] But from a slightly different perspective, Nazism and the Holocaust present, in Steiner's thought, an *occasion,* huge and monstrous, through which a largely repressed messianic sensibility can test itself, can come to know its faith and its doubts. It is only through such testing, even against the greatest inhumanities, that the humanistic spirit can justify its devotion to the ideal of culture. This becomes clear in the final paragraph of *Real Presences,* which draws upon both Christian and Jewish messianic motifs to produce the hushed anticipation of *tikkun:*

> But ours is the long day's journey of the Saturday. Between suffering, aloneness, unutterable waste on the one hand and the dream of liberation, of rebirth on the other. In the face of the torture of a child, of the death of love which is Friday, even the greatest art and poetry are almost helpless. In the Utopia of the Sunday, the aesthetic will, presumably, no longer have logic or necessity. The apprehensions and figurations in the play of metaphysical imagining, in the poem and the music, which tell of pain and of hope, of the flesh which is said to taste of ash and of the spirit which is said to have the savour of fire, are always Sabbatarian. They have risen out of an immensity of waiting which is that of man. Without them, how could we be patient?[25]

Here as elsewhere in the tradition, messianic thought is not only apocalyptic but utopian and restorative as well: it looks forward to an end and fulfillment of history, a world made anew, which is simultaneously the original, unfallen state of the past. Meanwhile, that which makes history bearable, because it is the site of the struggle between the ideal and the inhuman, is art, which would be understood in radically different terms with the fulfillment of the utopian or messianic promise. For Steiner, the way in which we choose to regard and understand art is of the utmost importance, for it reveals the way in which we choose to dwell in a "post-culture."

Given prevailing currents of thought, Steiner's own choice is a brave one, and may be regarded as a direct expression of the utopian dimension of his messianism:

> The thrust of will which engenders art and disinterested thought, the engaged response which alone can ensure its transmission to other human beings, to the future, are rooted in a gamble on transcendence. The writer or thinker means the words of the poem, the sinews of the argument, the personae of the drama, to outlast his own life, to take on the mystery of autonomous presence and presentness.[26]

Human creativity is a gamble on transcendence; human creation calls forth autonomous presence. Something is there in the artist's struggle to bring forth form; something is there in our encounter with the achieved work. The ground of belief has altered. Creeds and systems no longer have power over the modern mind, nurtured by skepticism (if not nihilism), but art, which has always partaken of mystery, maintains its power as transcendental witness. In the realm of the aesthetic we make our leap of faith:

> there is aesthetic creation because there is *creation*. There is formal construction because we have been made form.... The core of our human identity is nothing more or less than the fitful apprehension of the radically inexplicable presence, facticity and perceptible substantiality of the created. It is; we are. This is the rudimentary grammar of the unfathomable.[27]

This pronouncement can be readily understood, considering Steiner's heritage and his positions on related matters. As we have seen in regard to the problem of exile, Steiner can accept neither secular nor Orthodox attitudes. Although he feels himself to be cut off from ritual and systematic belief, he cannot bring himself to an understanding of culture that is totally desacralized. In this respect, he remains true to his modernist precursors such as Kafka and Benjamin, and feels obligated to struggle against the Postmodernism of such figures as Derrida. His answer to both the agony of modernism and the play of Postmodernism is a kind of sacred or theological aestheticism. Art does not replace religion, as Matthew Arnold had hoped, but rather, it is revealed to be the one enduring site of possible belief. When we encounter the poem, the painting, the symphony, there is a "knock at the door"; and in following the rules of courtesy, we admit the presence of the other. All secondary thought about art stems from the primal mystery of this encounter:

> The meaning, the existential modes of art, music and literature are functional within the experience of our meeting with the other. All aesthetics, all critical and hermeneutic discourse, is an attempt to clarify the paradox and opaqueness of that meeting as well as its felicities. The ideal of complete echo, of translucent reception is, exactly, that of the messianic. For the messianic dispensation, every semantic motion and marker would become perfectly intelligible truth; it would have the life-naming, life-giving authority of great art when it reaches the one for whom it is uniquely intended— and here, 'uniquely' does not mean 'solely'.[28]

The messianic tenor of this position has its counterpart, however, in just those strands of contemporary thought which Steiner hopes to resist. As he admits in his argument against the recent preponderance of critical theory, "I would define the claim to theory in the humanities as impatience systematized. Out of Judaism grown impatient at the everlasting delay of the messianic came strange fruit. Today, this impatience has taken on extreme, nihilistic urgency."[29] Thus, when Steiner addresses this systematized, nihilistic impatience, he is in effect addressing one logical outcome of the intellectual tradition to which he owes his allegiance. Indeed, his confrontation with critical theory (or at least with such masters as Derrida, Barthes, and De Man) is less of an argument than a rueful appreciation, from which he finally must turn away:

> *On its own terms and planes of argument,* terms by no means trivial if only in respect of their bracing acceptance of ephemerality and self-dissolution, the challenge of deconstruction does seem to me irrefutable. It embodies, it

ironizes into eloquence, the underlying nihilistic findings of literacy, of understanding or rather in-comprehension, as these *must* be stated in the time of the epilogue.[30]

To be sure, Steiner's theological assertion of "real presences" is totally irreconcilable with deconstructive celebrations of linguistic deferral and the absence of the sign. What we can say, however (and Steiner appears only partially conscious of this fact), is that these positions are complementary as well as antagonistic; in effect they represent the positive and negative moments in the contemporary history of messianic thought. Derrida, speaking in the spirit of apocalypse, announces the dissolution of "ontotheology" and the passage beyond humanism "in the formless, mute, infant, and terrifying form of monstrosity."[31] Steiner, the utopian humanist, asserts that there is no word less deconstructible than *hope.*

But in Steiner's vision, hope is continually assailed. Bound up in the idea of culture, and more specifically in what Steiner names in an early essay *humane literacy,* hope shudders and fades whenever the humanities prove incapable of resisting the inhuman. Humane literacy means total engagement with the work:

> In that great discourse with the living dead which we call reading, our role is not a passive one.... A great poem, a classic novel, press in upon us; they assail and occupy the strong places in our consciousness. They exercise upon our imagination and desires, upon our ambitions and most covert dreams, a strange, bruising mastery.[32]

This "bruising mastery" (and once again we encounter the rhetoric of power), however painful, is the guarantor of hope, the promise of handing down, of tradition, and therefore of futurity. But if traditions are passed down in the presence of horror, of utter spiritual and moral degradation, how then can hope avoid its deconstruction?

"To have heard Gieseking play the *Waldstein* in Munich, almost at the end. Despite brave efforts at ventilation smoke hung in the concert hall and an odor of fire and burst mains blew in through the gilt-and-stucco foyer."[33] This is the voice of Dr. Gervinus Rothling, the distinguished jurist and unrepentant ex-Nazi in *The Portage to San Cristobal of A. H.* A rigorously disciplined and orderly mind, learned in philosophy, history, and political science, and keenly appreciative of the nuanced world of music, Rothling is the fictional embodiment of the type which Steiner has invoked again and again: the man of culture and intelligence, steeped in the traditions of European humanism, who gave himself wholeheartedly to the Hitlerian vision. "He was true to his word," thinks Rothling, as he quietly listens to his daughter play Schumann. "A thousand-year Reich inside each of us, a millennium of remembered life." The appalling poetry of Rothling's reminiscences ("The sound and the fallen leaves came toward me down the dusky water. A moment out of time. Two bodies swinging high on the unbleached gallows by the roadside"), his majestic but somehow perverse meditation on music ("It sets itself across the general flow of time in which we conduct our regimented lives with a specific assertion of freedom so absolute as to dwarf other pretenses of liberty be they political, private, orgiastic") almost seduce us. We recall Steiner's speculation that certain types of cultural and intellectual achievement do not merely fail against the temptation of barbarism, but may actually incline the individual toward such a fall. "Is it reasonable to suppose that every high civilization will develop implosive stresses and impulses toward self-destruction?... Is the phenomenology of *ennui* and of a longing for violent dissolution a constant in the history of social and intellectual forms once they have passed a certain threshold of complication?"[34] These are the questions Steiner asks in his measured expository prose. "I Gervinus Rothling have emptied life not from a glass but from a magnum." So answers the author's creation.

The descent of European humanism into what Steiner calls "Hell made immanent" cannot be understood except in relation to the concomitant phenomenon of Western anti-Semitism. Steiner's thought on these matters is controversial in itself; as Alvin Rosenfeld notes, "Steiner challenged earlier arguments of both historical positivists and psychohistorians in an effort to get at what he believed to be some of the deeper cultural and religious strains of Nazism. There are those who have criticized this aspect of the author's thought as being too conjectural and others who have found it unusually bold and perceptive."[35] Complicating the issue immensely, however, is the fact that Steiner later incorporates his cultural criticism into his novel, especially in Hitler's monologue, which comprises its final chapter. But before we can evaluate this "translation," we must consider Steiner's theory in its expository form.

Like his more recent analysis of aesthetic experience, Steiner's examination of anti-Semitism and the Holocaust is based without apology upon the psychology of religion. As with the highest of human achievements, so with the most profound of human failures: civilization is best understood in terms of religious thought, regardless of whether the language of religion is regarded as metaphoric or as the human expression of transcendent truth. As far as I can see, Steiner is rather ambiguous on this issue. There are moments in *Real Presences* and *In Bluebeard's Castle* in which it seems that he employs religious discourse because its particular rhetorical qualities (its reservoir of archetypal symbols, its protean metaphors, its supple expression of subjectivity) make it the best instrument of cultural analysis. Steiner's insistence on the religious dimension of culture may be understood therefore as a means of achieving a particularly authoritative style, the expression of what I have already called his theological aestheticism.

But seen as either elaborate metaphor or flash of prophetic insight, there is no denying the vigor and invention of the analysis. However important we consider the economic, political, sociological, and psychological explanations of the Holocaust (and Steiner sees them as invaluable contributions), only the religious imagination and its unique vision of history can comprehend Western civilization's "season in Hell." In the course of Steiner's career, this imaginative force has shaped his work variously; a continuum of discourse, increasingly laden with risk, gradually unfolds.

"Postscript" (1966), one of the Holocaust essays in *Language and Silence,* offers a severe but nonetheless fairly safe position:

> What the Nazis did in the camps and torture chambers is wholly unforgivable, it is a brand on the image of man and will last; each of us has been diminished by the enactment of a potential sub-humanity latent in all of us. But if one did not undergo the thing, hate and forgiveness are spiritual games— serious games no doubt—but games none the less. The best *now,* after so much has been set forth, is, perhaps, to be silent, not to add the trivia of literary, sociological debate to the unspeakable. So argues Elie Wiesel, so argued a number of witnesses at the Eichmann trial. The next best is, I believe, to try and understand, to keep faith with what may well be the utopian commitment to reason and historical analysis...[36]

Here, the individual who has not personally experienced Nazi atrocity can decently confront the Holocaust only with a kind of religious silence and a clerical devotion to the witnessing work of those who were there. Even Steiner himself, "a kind of survivor," can only produce acts of remembrance, a *kaddish* (this is how he will come to regard "Lieber's Lament" from *The Portage* as well). But *In Bluebeard's Castle* (1971) represents a shift in perspective. Brooding once again upon the Holocaust, Steiner declares that "I am not sure whether anyone, however scrupulous, who spends time and imaginative resources on these dark places can or, indeed, ought to leave them personally intact. Yet the dark places are at the center. Pass them by and there can be no serious discussion of the human potential."[37] He then launches into his controversial psychotheological hypothesis, parts of which are then woven into the fiction of *The Portage* some years later. The continuum from silence and remembrance through exposition and speculation to literary representation is thus shot through with reversals and revisions—but this is in no way meant as criticism. If we are indeed fascinated, perhaps even corrupted by what constitutes for Steiner "a second Fall," then we must struggle against the existential burden of post-Holocaust life with every means at our disposal.

Steiner's pervasive sense that the Holocaust is both the culmination of a historical dialectic and the hellish entrance into our contemporary time of the "after-Word" is best explained in *In Bluebeard's Castle*. He hypothesizes that the original "invention" of monotheism and its adoption by the Jews proved to be an intolerable affront and challenge to Western civilization, secure in the natural immanence of polytheism and animism. Totally abstract, absolutely without image, and utterly dedicated to the Sinaic concept of justice, the God of Moses, once revealed, refused to be denied:

> To all but a very few the Mosaic God has been from the outset, even when passionately invoked, an immeasurable Absence, or a metaphor modulating downward to the natural sphere of poetic imagistic approximation. But the exaction stays in force—immense, relentless. It hammers at human consciousness, demanding that it transcend itself, that it reach out into a light of understanding so pure that it is itself blinding. We turn back into grossness, and what is more important, into self-reproach.[38]

As history takes its course, this Jewish ideal is revised twice, each time with no less sense of the absolute: in primitive Christianity,

with its insistence on "sacrificial self-denial," and in messianic socialism, with its "magnetic" dream of utopian plenitude. In each case,
abstract, implacable justice serves as the guiding principle. As Steiner
says, "Unceasingly, the blackmail of perfection has hammered at the
confused, mundane, egotistical fabric of common, instinctual behavior."[39] And when the essentially Jewish demand for perfection upon
the consciousness of the West grew unbearable,

> Deep loathing built up in the social subconscious, murder-
> ous resentments. The mechanism is simple but primordial.
> *We hate most those who hold out to us a goal, an ideal, a
> visionary promise which, even though we have stretched our
> muscles to the utmost, we cannot reach, which slips, again and
> again, just out of range of our racked fingers—yet, and this is
> crucial, which remains profoundly desirable, which we cannot
> reject because we fully acknowledge its supreme value.* In his
> exasperating "strangeness," in his acceptance of suffering as
> part of a covenant with the absolute, the Jew became, as it
> were, the "bad conscience of Western history."[40]

The result is not merely the death of God, but the attempted annihilation of His people—"an attempt to level the future—or, more precisely, to make history commensurate with the natural savageries,
intellectual torpor, and material instincts of unextended man."[41]
Hell, long envisioned in graphic detail by the Western imagination, is
made manifest in the camps.

This awful, elegant theory demonstrates Steiner's messianism to
the fullest extent. Steiner chooses to label the Holocaust a second Fall,
but the aura that surrounds his meditation is surely apocalyptic. For
the earlier generation of Jewish messianists, apocalypse, with its "complete destruction and negation of the old order," produces "a quan-
tum leap from present to future, from exile to freedom."[42] But Steiner, following after and attempting to explain the Holocaust, perceives
an apocalypse that has gone terribly awry: destruction and negation
have not cleansed civilization (as would be the case in an idealized
Marxist revolution) but have besmirched it. Apocalyptic violence does
not usher in utopia but signifies an atavistic return of primal brutality,
what in theological terms could only be considered total corruption
and sin. Instead of a rupture with profane history, a clean break with
the past, humanity fails the test of transcendence, and history, a long
passage of spiritual suppuration interspersed with unbearable ethical

demands, discharges its vile load. And because we can now accept the catastrophic fact that human nature is capable of *anything* (a concept which has horrified and outraged Steiner throughout his career), we cannot build a New Jerusalem, but must face, rather, the interminable banality, the permanent decline, of life in a "post-culture."

We are now in a position to consider *The Portage* as the most recent stage (I hesitate to say the last) of Steiner's long engagement with the inhuman. A great deal has already been written about the novel, and I do not propose to offer here a complete interpretation of the text. Rather, my concern is with the terms of the debate which have arisen over the work and their significance to my reading of Steiner's vision of Judaism and Western culture.

The argument must be carefully framed. Those who have attacked *The Portage* complain that Steiner's manipulation of ideas in key passages (including those from his own essays), culminating in Hitler's speech, produces moral ambiguity if not actual excuses for Nazi anti-Semitism. The fact that Hitler has "the last word" in the text especially frustrates these critics. As Alvin Rosenfeld says, "To close the novel on this note is to succumb, rhetorically, to the seductive eloquence of negation, a closure that appeals to the very same instincts courted with such devastating effect by Hitler himself."[43] On the other hand, Robert Boyers contends that most critics read *The Portage* as an expository presentation of ideas and fail to comprehend it as a work of fiction. According to Boyers, we must remember

> to consider the structure of the narrative, the way in which certain characters are so placed as to challenge, or at least implicitly compromise, the assertions of others, the way in which the irony works...to frame and set a limit to the dizzier philosophical ruminations that otherwise dominate the novel. The ideas expressed in *The Portage* are not, after all, what they would be, what indeed they are, in the pages of various critical and philosophical works. They are not espoused but presented as a part of the material the novelist wishes to bring before us.... Nowhere does the novel forget that it is a novel, and nowhere does it instruct us to read as if the ideas were themselves both object and motive of the narrative.[44]

Boyers's sensitivity to matters of form serves as an important corrective to those readers who, when confronted with a novel of ideas, immediately transfer moral and political attitudes from the aesthetic structure to the social arena, seeking to ascribe one or another position to the author. This is not to say that by writing fiction Steiner is freed of responsibility for the ideas in the work. On the contrary, these ideas bear upon our political decisions and moral judgments with great force—but in a unique, highly mediated fashion which we must try to understand in each of our encounters with a work of literature. The conditions which *The Portage* imposes upon us, its mediating formalisms, are taxing in the extreme:

> It was only a step, gentlemen, a small, inevitable step, from Sinai to Nazareth, from Nazareth to the covenant of Marxism....
>
> Three times the Jew has pressed on us the blackmail of transcendence. Three times he has infected our blood and brains with the bacillus of perfection. Go to your rest and the voice of the Jew cries out in the night: "Wake up! God's eye is upon you. Has He not made you in His image? Lose your life so that you may gain it. Sacrifice yourself to the truth, to justice, to the good of mankind." That cry had been in our ears too long, gentlemen, far too long. Men had grown sick of it, sick to death.[45]

This, of course, is Steiner's Hitler, offering a parody of Steiner's own ideas—a parody produced less by twisting the original ideas (though Hitler does that too) than by situating them in a speech in which he explains and defends his actions. Yet this cannot be called self-parody in the conventional sense of the term. As Boyers understands, when studying Steiner's ideas in the novel, context counts for as much as content:

> Hitler's grammar of hell, as brought before us in a living language, should be able to appropriate and invert any sacred terminology, including one originally invented—by Steiner himself, in previous essays and books—to express a combination of horror, guilt, inadequacy, and sheer driven disquietude in the face of a historical event that remains "indivisible" from his own identity.... The final speech demonstrates that a Hitler can appropriate a Steiner for his purposes by willfully ignoring, and thus violating, the spirit and intent of Steiner's original utterances and turning them to totally alien purposes.[46]

This interpretation may not satisfy those readers who expect a definitive moral statement to present itself upon the conclusion of a given novel, especially one as morally fraught as *The Portage to San Cristobal of A. H.* Moral judgments are manifest throughout the book in both form and content, and lead us to moral judgments of our own: but they are not to be found in *The Portage* as they are in *Language and Silence* or *In Bluebeard's Castle.* Steiner has too much respect for the power of the aesthetic, too much intimate knowledge of its dangers, and far too much novelistic skill, not to allow his work its full charge of ethical vexation. If we are truly to comprehend the depravity of Hitler's anti-Semitism, then, like the Israeli team in the Amazon (or like Marlow, their great precursor in *Heart of Darkness*), we must experience what Boyers calls Hitler's "power of transvaluation"—knowing full well how perilously akin this ideological power is to that of fiction itself. As Terry Eagleton explains,

> Ideology signifies the imaginary ways in which men experience the real world, which is, of course, the kind of experience literature gives us too—what it feels like to live in particular conditions, rather than a conceptual analysis of those conditions. However, art does more than just passively reflect that experience. It is held within ideology, but also manages to distance itself from it, to the point where it permits us to 'feel' and 'perceive' the ideology from which it springs.[47]

It is especially important to keep this modus operandi in mind when interpreting a work like *The Portage,* which ambiguously represents an extreme and repugnant ideology, and one which is itself capable of distorting historical and psychological insights.

The notorious conclusion of *The Portage* is thus even less conclusive than it first appears, in accord with the messianic tenor of Steiner's thought. The entire novel is shot through with messianic references, especially Lieber's and Elie Barach's considerations of Hitler as an anti-messiah, one who has mastered the grammar of hell, God's counterlanguage of evil and negation. Speaking of the Holocaust and the birth of Israel, A. H. too mockingly says "Perhaps I *am* the Messiah, the true Messiah, the new Sabbatai whose infamous deeds were allowed by God in order to bring His people home."[48] These remarks help to establish the position of individual speakers and convey Steiner's conviction that only a highly charged theological discourse, an apocalyptic language, can do justice to his themes. Yet Steiner's messianism runs deepest not in any allusion or reference but in the way the novel unblinkingly poses questions of ultimate evil and justice. As the work unfolds, with chapters focusing on the Israelis interspersed with chapters revealing the thoughts and responses of the various national types confronting the growing possibility of A. H.'s reality, we are gradually prepared for the apocalyptic moment of Hitler's speech, a moment when finally we are able to hear this language of negation, whatever the risk. As is the case with *In Bluebeard's Castle,* we face a terrible reversal of transcendental justice and the most excruciating of human failures. But in *The Portage* we do not simply understand this disaster as we do in Steiner's criticism; we experience its representation.

Nevertheless, even this disastrous moment, which some have read as an ironic triumph for Nazism in Steiner's work, remains radically open. Saul Friedlander, in what is perhaps the most subtle critique of the novel, implicates Steiner in "the new discourse about Nazism," what he calls "a kitsch of the apocalypse."[49] According to Friedlander, *The Portage,* like the other recent books and films which he examines (and unlike *Language and Silence*), is a dangerous work because it aestheticizes and thereby neutralizes some of the worst aspects of Nazism. "Eloquence," says Friedlander, "the real eloquence of the pseudo-Hitler—may reach deeply into those murky labyrinths of present day fantasies about Nazism or the Jews."[50]

Compelling and important as Friedlander's general argument is, I still believe that Steiner is justified in the risks taken by his novel. As we have seen, Steiner has long been aware of the dangers involved in dealing with Holocaust material, yet believes that no responsible artist or critic can avoid them. Furthermore, Steiner's apocalyptic sensibility is, arguably, free of the element of kitsch which Friedlander accurately locates in work such as Michel Tournier's *The Ogre* or the memoirs of Albert Speer. Jewish messianism, including Steiner's, is never merely a matter of apocalyptic destruction, which in itself can certainly be perverted into a kitsch of death. Apocalyptic but still lacking the debased romanticism of annihilation, messianic works, including *The Portage,* partake equally in the openness of utopian thought.

The Portage does not end with Hitler's speech. As Joseph Lowin has pointed out, the monologue is followed by the appearance of the helicopters. We do not know who has sent them nor what they will do: "The answer one gives to the question raised by the hovering helicopters is in part determined by one's *Weltanschau-ung,* by one's vision of the world."[51] Thus, in midrashic fashion, the text casts its problem back upon the reader; it calls for the very dialogue (or dispute) which it has in fact provoked. While Hitler's triumph, his final perversion of justice, must be considered a possibility—and an apocalyptic sensibility might accept, might even welcome such a horror—this is only one of an endless number of conclusions, given the indeterminacy of the text and the open range of reader responses.

Tishbi yetzaretz kushyot ve'abayot: the messiah will answer questions and problems. In the Talmud, the phrase denotes the contradiction or inconclusiveness of an argument which cannot be resolved. The answer is infinitely deferred, and with it the satisfaction that comes of intellectual or formal closure. It appears as an acronym: *teku,* a word which in modern Hebrew means a tie score.[52] It is, of course, the name Steiner gives to the Indian who is chosen as the witness in A. H.'s trial, who despite the fact that he cannot understand Hitler's words is about to cry out "Proved" just before the helicopters break up the proceedings. His name, charged with an aura of ancient learning, bears within its small span the radical doubt and radical faith that we have come to associate with George Steiner's entire career.

▲

CHAPTER 7

Walter Benjamin, Messianism, and Marxism: A Midrash

The process of the soul's connection with the body—called the "descent of the soul into matter"—is, from a certain perspective, the soul's profound tragedy. But the soul undertakes this terrible risk as a part of the need to descend in order to make the desired ascent to hitherto unknown heights. It is a risk and a danger, because the soul's connection with the body and its contact with the material world where it is the only factor that is free— unbounded by the determinism of physical law and able to choose and move freely—make it possible for the soul to fall and, in falling, to destroy the world. Indeed, Creation itself, and the creation of man, is precisely such a risk, a descent for the sake of ascension.[1]

I

It has often been observed that since the onset of Romanticism, the fragment, self-contained but fraught with absence, has been granted a privileged status in literature and, to some extent, in philosophy. Even Marx, endlessly fascinated by Hegel's system-building, produces that most Nietzschean set of aphorisms, the *Theses on Feuerbach*. Modernism, perhaps a more formal and self-conscious movement, misreads the ubiquitous presence of the Romantic fragment and transforms it into a definite cultural project. We think of *Ulysses* and *The Waste Land,* of Kafka and Brecht, of Schoenberg and *Mini-*

ma Moralia. Walter Benjamin, student of monads, theorist of dialectic at a standstill, naturally belongs in this great company. In his essay on Surrealism, moving with concerted effort away from his early theological orientation toward a profane critical stance, he calls for the possession of the image sphere "in which political materialism and physical nature share the inner man, the psyche, the individual, or whatever else we wish to throw to them, with dialectical justice, so that no limb remains unrent."[2] Here, as much as in Brecht's epic theater, we see the aggressive assertion of a left-wing modernist program with studious fragmentation placed strategically at its heart.

That Jewish messianism and all its mystical baggage should be a crucial component in this program remains as potentially scandalous today as when Benjamin debated with Scholem, Adorno, and Brecht. Perhaps this is because the contradictions inherent in Benjamin's work remain as vexing as they ever were. On the other hand, it can also be said of Benjamin that theological thought, as it infects historical materialism—and vice versa—is quite compatible with the form as well as the content of the body of its intellectual host. Surely the *Theses on the Philosophy of History,* a gnomic masterpiece of modernist technique, can also be read as a midrash, turning and turning the messianic idea under the black light of history. The resulting constellation, sealing Benjamin's canon as it permanently problematizes his materialist version of redemptive criticism, also opens itself provocatively to the continuum of commentary that is the sine qua non of the Jewish textual tradition. What Scholem calls the "religious dignity" of commentary is transferred to the profane ground of materialist speculation: what is produced is an uncanny form as ridden by doubt and hope as any of Kafka's parables.

Because we have learned to distrust totality and the affirmation of presence, knowledge of this sort can only apprehend itself through the midrashic and kabbalistic techniques so strangely rediscovered by modernism. The peculiar constellation made up of messianism, Marxism, and secular literature can only be addressed through fragmentary theses and the radical juxtaposition of discrete texts. Thus Benjamin becomes an exemplary figure not only for critical theory but for modern Jewish culture as well.

II

In Benjamin's first thesis, historical materialism is a bold automaton, theology a wizened dwarf inhabiting its interior and controlling its movement. Rolf Tiedemann, commenting on this allegory of the chess player, frames the dilemma in a most orderly fashion:

> A paradoxical situation is produced in Benjamin's thesis regarding the relationship between historical materialism and theology. In order to be able to catch up with real history again, historical materialism must return *beyond* philosophy to *theology*. Granted, it is still historical materialism that "is to win," but to be *able* to win, it is to require the services of the most spiritual of all disciplines. The question remains, whether Benjamin's attempt was successful; whether the alliance of historical materialism and theology is actually able to produce a new unity of theory and practice.[3]

But perhaps the question is not one of *success* but of definitions—and of priorities. Neither scholarship nor speculation has provided a clear view of our critical goals: we do not understand what it is we seek to understand. The fragments are compiled, the theories concocted, but the "new unity" remains as problematic as ever. In what would such unity consist? Did Benjamin, who knowingly took the risk of becoming a messianic Marxist, ever desire it? Do we?

III

For the critic, one of the most important questions arising from the dubious alliance of theology and historical materialism may be posed rather bluntly: what does it mean to "redeem" the text? From a Marxist perspective, shouldn't the text remain in a permanently infected, that is, secularized and contradictory condition? On the other hand, when the text is trapped in the realm of *Das Immergleiche,* of "homogeneous, empty time" which Benjamin invokes throughout the *Theses,* do we have any choice but to "rescue" it? In regard to "saving the text," Marxism and messianism are structurally analogous, except that in the end the analogy always breaks down: the secular desire for human liberation reasserts itself as theology continues to peer upward in its attempt to pierce the veil of the heavens. After all, it is the Marxist puppet that is to win the worldly chess game all the time—though some have rightly come to question the nature of its victory.

In his absorbing study of Benjamin's "aesthetic of redemption," Richard Wolin observes that:

> In the end, Benjamin's redemptive criticism had become thoroughly profane. It ceased to concern itself with presenting an image of otherworldly truth. Instead, its task became one of emancipating cultural products from the debilitating grip of ideological falsification and thereby rendering their truths serviceable for the impending revolutionary transformation of society.[4]

Perhaps. But even when redemptive criticism becomes thoroughly profane, dealing exclusively with material phenomena, it still remains redemptive and hence always concerned with presenting if not otherworldly truth than at least a metaphysical representation. Marxism is *always already* theological. The critic must remain perpetually vigilant: ideological falsification is a constant threat of extraordinary subtlety, and even claims about culture made in the name of an impending revolution are by no means immune to such reification. As Benjamin himself says, "The concept of progress should be grounded in the idea of catastrophe. That things 'just keep on going' *is* the catastrophe. Not something that is impending at any particular time ahead, but something that is always given."[5]

This radical anti-historicism, leading, of course, to the vision of the angel in the ninth thesis, stands as a warning against any complacent deconstruction leading to a self-assured rescue. Each fissure discovered in the text simultaneously mends it. And just as there is no document of civilization which is not at the same time a document of barbarism, there is no rescue of the text from the march of "progress" which is not at the same time a reinsertion of the text into that same procession.

IV

In *The Messianic Idea in Judaism,* Gershom Scholem writes:

> There is something grand about living in hope, but at the same time something profoundly unreal about it. It diminishes the singular worth of the individual, and he can never fulfill himself, because the incompleteness of his endeavors eliminates precisely what constitutes its highest value. Thus in Judaism the Messianic idea has compelled a *life lived in deferment,* in which nothing can be done definitively, nothing can be irrevocably accomplished.[6]

Perhaps it is at this point that Scholem's work and that of his friend
Walter Benjamin come into the closest proximity. Certainly the function of Jewish messianism in Benjamin's thought finds a precise articulation here. Messianism allows him to move through, or better, to dis-
place the double bind of rescue and reification, of dialectical image and
cultural monument, in which he would otherwise be caught. Work
done (life lived) in deferment means that the text upon which the critic
operates is always being placed at a distance; as Benjamin says of the
Arcades Project, "In order for a part of the past to be touched by the
present, there must be no continuity between them." The provisional
quality of even Benjamin's most authoritative criticism (such as the late
essays on Leskov, Kafka, and Baudelaire) arises from just this fortunate
discontinuity, which obtains for contemporary phenomena as surely as
for those of the past. The critic encounters the text at a messianic distance, aware of the unreality or incompleteness of an endeavor in
which every second of time might be "the strait gate through which
the Messiah might enter." Critical discourse is thus cast in the condi-
tional; it seeks to "de-territorialize" its assertions at every turn. Likewise, it is anti-hagiographic: though Benjamin and his subjects are now
canonized, within his own writing he resists canonization as strenuously as he can. Deferment too is a kind of redemption.

This is not to say that Benjamin fulfills himself despite his
endeavors' obvious incompleteness. Rather, when historical materialism is cast in messianic colors, fulfillment must be redefined. It
becomes a function of the negative, to be found, as it were, in the
gap between rescue and reification. Marx speaks of the moment
when the theories of the philosophers become the intellectual
weapons of the masses. For Benjamin, it is a moment of both dread
and exaltation (for Scholem, the student of Shabbetai Zevi, it is simply a disaster). And in this double bind there can be no displacement.

V

At this point we must take note of some troubling circumstances.
Jacob Neusner takes issue with Scholem on the subject of Jewish
messianism, asserting that "the Messianic Idea in Judaism" is in itself
a most misleading formulation. In his exhaustive study of the foundations of Judaism, Neusner declares:

>   ...Scholem provide[s] portraits of a composite that, in fact,
>   never existed in any one book, time, or place, or in the imag-

ination of any one social group, except an imagined "Israel" or a made-up "Judaism."

Once we distinguish one type or system of Judaism or one group of Israelites from another, recognizing commonalities and underscoring points of difference, we no longer find it possible to describe and analyze *the* messianic idea at all. Indeed, in the present context, we can no longer even comprehend the parallel categories, *the...idea,* and *in Judaism.*[7]

Neusner's disagreement with Scholem is part of a larger dispute between a normative view of Judaism and one infused with a sense of anarchic "counterhistory." As such, the claims of both sides must be scrupulously judged by all who heed the call to remembrance and are *observant of history.* Permit me, then, a radical argument: the historical validity of Scholem's messianic idea is irrelevant to our present purposes. The care with which Benjamin produces his dialectical images, his valiant research that brushes history against the grain, that moment of danger when the true picture of the past flits by—in short, all the *poetry* of his theoretical formulations—mutely gesture to the critical fiction under construction upon a messianic foundation. It is the nature of this construction we examine herein, with hopes of retracing its blueprints.

"The Messiah will come only when he is no longer necessary; he will come, not on the last day, but on the very last." Even if Benjamin did not get to read that particular aphorism of Kafka, he was implicitly aware of it and took it to heart. The messianic idea inspires the critical project of the historical materialist but also stands outside of it. Nor should one try to imagine that very last day, when the messianic underpinnings are no longer necessary, when the dwarf slips away and the automaton keeps winning his games: it is forbidden.

VI

Because we cannot dispense with the messianic foundation of Marxist criticism, but still seek a more refined understanding of the relationship, we turn inevitably from theology and epistemology to the sociology of knowledge. In his study of secular Jewish intellectuals, John Cuddihy observes that Marx transforms Jewry's "ordeal of civility" as European Jews anxiously attempt to assimilate into gentile culture into the universal dialectic of recognizable material self-interest and the deceptively false consciousness of ideolgy. Cuddihy also notes that "With Jewish secularization-modernization...Judasim is psychologized into Jewishness, and the personal Messiah is deperson-alized."[8] Among assimilated Jewish thinkers, the persistent need to maintain intellectual and emotional ties to messianic belief results, in the case of Marx, with the privileged status of the proletariat and the indescribable realm of freedom which will proceed from the wither-ing of the state. Thus Jurgen Habermas, in his essay celebrating Ger-shom Scholem, traces a movement from kabbalistic messianism to "a messianic activism that ultimately takes on the more profane meaning of a political liberation from exile. From the early Marx on down to Bloch and the late Benjamin, it takes the form of 'no resurrection of nature without a revolutionizing of society.'"[9]

But the dissolution of the personal messiah, only partially recon-stituted in the profane struggle for political liberation, remains a palpa-ble influence on those cultural critics who trace their descent back to Marx. We know the effect of the Hitler-Stalin pact on Benjamin's thought during the last months of his life. Perhaps this is only the most extreme example of a pervasive response to the frustration of political aspirations of left-wing European intellectuals in the early to mid part of the century: a response which remains the inheritance of leftist thinkers in developed Western countries today. As transformed mes-sianic hopes are thwarted or crushed in the political sphere, the cultur-al sphere takes on greater importance both symbolically and in terms of praxis. The redeemed text revealed in the critic's discourse stands in for the revolutionized society which failed to appear in the course of history. Indeed, in the ongoing present, when nought but immediacy prevails, criticism's redemption of the text allows for an appearance of messianic plenitude that can be experienced personally, subjectively, inwardly. "We begin empty" says Ernst Bloch as he starts *The Principle of Hope,* and we are progressively filled in the course of that great work; our individual capacity gradually achieved as interpretation ren-ders utopian the content of culture. Benjamin, in more straitened cir-cumstances, anticipates a redeemed humankind receiving the fullness of its past, but is himself granted only "chips of messianic time."

VII

Those who continue to be caught up in the trajectory I have been describing also continue to run much the same risks. Commenting on the debate between Benjamin and Adorno, Richard Wolin makes the following contrast:

> For Benjamin theory possesses an inalienable constructive or redemptive function; for Adorno its task is to aid in the ideology-critical unveiling of socially engendered false consciousness—if it should attempt to do anything more than this, it runs the risk of providing illusory consolation for real historical suffering.[10]

But if the redemption of the text runs the risk of providing illusory consolation for real historical suffering, it may also provide access to a kind of knowledge which cannot be achieved through any other critical procedure. Such knowledge is prefigurative and essentially poetic, keeping in mind Hannah Arendt's insight that Benjamin *thought poetically.* The image-worlds of poetry derive their authority from their totally synthetic nature: poetry draws upon prevailing historical and linguistic circumstances as they operate within an individual psyche, producing a text that is simultaneously contingent and autonomous. Poetry (like Marx's universal class) is a subject-object; it appropriates and transforms the constituent elements of its world in order to produce itself, but at the same time it acts upon itself, knowing that it is the chief element in its production. Redemptive criticism, which for Benjamin is always marked by the production of dialectical images, offers its knowledge in precisely the same manner.

In his study of Benjamin, Terry Eagleton observes the striking similarity between Adorno's critical methods and those of deconstruction in their shared "rage against positivity, the suspicion of determinate meaning *as such,* the fear that to propose is to be complicit."[11] Benjamin, it would appear, remains less taken with matters of negativity and difference. Instead, texts

> figure for him less as expressive media than as material ceremonies, scriptive fields of force to be negotiated, dense dispositions of signs less to be 'read' than meditatively engaged, incanted, and ritually re-made. As non-intentional constellations, texts may be deciphered only by the equally 'sacred' pursuits of critique and commentary, in which a language similarly unleashed from intention into its material fullness may catch in its net of mutual resonances something of the 'idea', the pattern of diverse significations, of the text it studies.[12]

As Eagleton understands, this leads us back past Marxism to Benjamin's theological roots, for Benjamin, despite his Marxism—and despite Scholem's judgment thereupon—is no heretic. Benjamin's faith in the revelatory power of commentary, which can consist as often of the reconstructive constellations or juxtapositions of fragmented texts as of direct interpretive discourse, shows us just how literal, how free of metaphor, the notion of redemption remains in his work.

In his desire to blast open the continuum of history, securing a messianic cessation of happening through the abrupt appearance of a dialectical image, Benjamin seeks for *tikkun* or restoration, despite his obvious fascination with the destructive character. As he says in his brief essay defining that figure, "The destructive character knows only one watchword: make room; only one activity: clearing away."[13] As Eagleton would have it, the machismo of the historical materialist's notorious refusal of the whore called "Once upon a time" enables him to violate or "blast open" the virgin of history. But this feminist interpretation should be augmented by a kabbalistic reading: the destructive historical materialist is an agent of *tzimtzum,* the withdrawal of God that opens a space wherein creation may unfold. In the Lurianic Kabbalah, the subsequent "breaking of the vessels," the cosmic catastrophe which leads to our own fallen world, inevitably impels the faithful to "raise the sparks," the shards of emanated light from the broken creation. Through their obedience to the Torah, religious Jews participate in the gradual process of universal redemption. Equally obedient to the text, Benjamin ceremoniously forms constellations which raise the sparks of the broken image-worlds, setting them in renewed patterns so that their messianic potential for liberation may be seen. Against the dull background of historicism's *Immergleich,* these interpretive patterns suddenly shine forth, positive images born out of violence and negation. And if history is like a woman, then she must be none other than the Shekinah, who suffers in Exile but may likewise be redeemed through devotion to the text.

VIII

It is good to put a truncated end to materialistic investigations.[14]

December 22, 1989. While American troops are fighting in Panama, in Rumania the people have swept one of the last Stalinist dictators in

Europe out of power. The most dismal and the most hopeful decade since the end of World War II comes to a close with the United States still rehearsing its old imperialistic ways in Latin America and the countries of Eastern Europe daring to create their own future. Who can safely speak of Marxism or messianism now? What texts are calling for redemption? Who dares pronounce upon the past when in moments of crisis, *even the dead* are not safe? Nor is there a clear-cut enemy, as there was when Benjamin wrote his *Theses*. Instead, we must content ourselves with a different sort of heroism.

▲

Chapter 8

Nostalgia and Futurity: Jewish Literature in Transition

In Philip Roth's "The Prague Orgy," the epilogue to *Zuckerman Bound,* there is an extraordinary passage which sums up the state of contemporary Jewish writing in the Diaspora, at least as I have constructed it in this book. It is 1976, and the hapless Nathan Zuckerman has gone to Prague on a secret mission: he intends to rescue the manuscript of stories written by the father of the half-Jewish émigré author Zdenek Sisovsky, whom Zuckerman has met in New York. These stories, written in "the Yiddish of Flaubert," are presently in the possession of Olga, Sisovsky's embittered, half-crazy, and outrageously promiscuous ex-wife, a woman who, despite her obvious attraction to Zuckerman, could lead him into a disastrous entanglement with the Czech authorities. Frustrated by his encounters with Olga, trailed by police agents, Zuckerman loses his way in the old city of Prague. Wandering about the "tunneled alleys and medieval streets," Zuckerman recalls how "as a Hebrew-school student of little more than nine" he would go from house to house collecting money for the Jewish National Fund, dreaming of the "used city" that the Jews would be able to buy with the nickels and dimes he gathered. The decay of the Czech capital, both picturesque and miserable to the eye of the affluent American writer, reminds him of his imaginary Jewish homeland—not Palestine, where "hearty Jewish teenagers" are busy "reclaiming the desert and draining the swamps," but an Old World town, archaic and dilapidated, where nothing is produced but stories:

all the telling and listening to be done, their infinite interest in their own existence, the fascination with their alarming plight, the mining and refining of *tons* of these stories—the national industry of the Jewish homeland, if not the sole means of production (if not the sole source of satisfaction), the construction of narratives out of the exertions of survival.[1]

Despite Roth's usually more caustic attitude, it is one more version of the textual homeland, as suffused with nostalgia as any of the formulations we have encountered up until now—Bloom's patriarchal agon, Steiner's autistic clerics, Mandelbaum's pedantic Chelm, Ozick's Schulzian messiah. And of course, Benjamin's aura, that light filling an impossible distance as the past, with all its stories, recedes from view.

In all these instances, linguistic production, this "national industry of the Jewish homeland," comes to be associated with loss and deprivation. There was a time when the Jews, however much they suffered in exile, were able to master their verbal circumstances to such an extent that they could dwell in the Word, buoyed up in an endless stream of discourse as bountiful as Scholem's Ur-Torah from which God read to begin the original ritual of creation. But that time is gone. For the poets, the unifying symbol is lost, and the play of words offers little compensation. For the critics, the obsessive text-centeredness of an intellectual elite gives way before the blandishments of popular culture. For the novelists, the cultural authority of the tale is broken and the narrative splinters or turns in upon itself. The Jewish writer may be more secure, but that very security counts for very little except, perhaps, the writer's actual decline in literary strength. In every case, the current act of writing is marked by the imagination of past wholeness, a melancholy longing for irretrievable conditions that were somehow more conducive to the writer's task, and a nagging sense of diminishment or inadequacy. The work, in short, is premised upon nostalgic remembrance. Like Benjamin's angel, it is always looking backward toward Paradise, from which a disastrous wind hurtles it into the future.

Let us return to Zuckerman in Prague. How is Zuckerman's quest a matter of nostalgia? How is Roth's presentation of that quest likewise nostalgic? And most importantly, how does nostalgia further Roth's literary ends, making not only "The Prague Orgy" but all of his recent works such riotous, soul-searching reflections of the contemporary Jewish consciousness? For surely Roth's goal in the passage with which we began is to represent a critical, emblematic moment for that consciousness, one acutely aware of itself as divorced from Old World Jewish traditions and doubtful of the modern attitudes and institutions which have taken their place.

In Zuckerman's second-hand city (the description is somewhat reminiscent of Bruno Schulz's vision of Drohobycz in *The Street of Crocodiles*), "What you smell are centuries and what you hear are voices and what you see are Jews, wild with lament and rippling with amusement." But these Jews with their jokes and stories, barely getting by on the margins of European society, are really a "Jewish Atlantis of an American childhood dream"; their existence in Zuckerman's imagination is a measure of both the living reality of the Jewish past and its inexorable distance from secular Jewish life in the present. Zuckerman, the modern Jew, is linked to the past by his particular linguistic abilities: his mordant wit, his dialogic subtlety, his vivid storytelling imagination. Indeed, it is through these very powers, which he believes he has inherited, that he creates a nostalgic version of the enduring Jewish traditions of narrative, humor, and verbal tenacity in the face of disaster. As Gershom Scholem says, speaking of innovation in the development of sacred Jewish textuality, "The desire for historical continuity which is of the very essence of tradition is translated into a historical construction whose fictitious character cannot be doubted but which serves the believing mind as a crutch of external authentication."[2] But in the modern case of Zuckerman (and Roth), the tradition is understood to be a fictional construction; hence their doubt regarding its ultimate strength to endure. Nostalgia for a discursive tradition becomes, in effect, the fuel for the new work of the imagination.

The stories which Zuckerman hopes to retrieve were written by a man described by his son as having "belonged to nothing," a man suffering from "homelessness beyond homelessness," an author even more homeless than Kafka. Among his tales is "Mother Tongue," "Three pages only, about a little Jewish boy who speaks bookish German, Czech without the native flavor, and the Yiddish of people simpler than himself."[3] The son, Zdenek Sisovsky, may not be trustworthy, but his account of the father's life, death, and secret literary achievement, is enough to inspire Zuckerman's quest. (This is, of course, the same Zuckerman who has lived through the monstrous physical comedy, the somatic crisis of faith of *The Anatomy Lesson*.) Everything about the situation, from the father's Gentile wife (whose presence always reminds him of his Jewishness) to his murder by the Gestapo (a death which the son may be inventing, drawing on the famous shooting of Bruno Schulz), to Zdenek himself (whose identity as an émigré writer persecuted by the Czech Communist regime evokes envy in his new American friend) seems tailormade for Zuckerman, who seeks links with his Jewish literary past which will also help him distinguish his own Jewish identity in the present. Yet that Jewish past, as symbolized by the manuscript which Olga finally gives him, is literally inscrutable: Zuckerman, the typical American Jew, cannot read Yiddish. When the stories are confiscated by the Czech police, one feels as if the brute hand of History itself is breaking the chain of Jewish culture which Zuckerman hopes to keep intact. But this is hardly a matter of tragedy: as Zuckerman himself observes just before his last encounter with Olga, it is a case of *"The soul sinking into ridiculousness even while it strives to be saved."*[4] What Roth knows, what Zuckerman and the reader learn, is that Jewish homelessness, endlessly reinforced by such tragicomic episodes as these, is just what furthers Jewish devotion to the text. However ridiculous the modern Jew appears (and in his alien enthusiasms, is he any more or less ridiculous than his Old World forebears?), devotion to the Word remains the test of his faith.

In the hands of a Jewish author like Roth, nostalgia is not merely a mood which hovers about the work; it partakes in a more or less conscious literary strategy, a means of furthering the task of writing and of making a place for oneself in the tradition, or as Harold Bloom would say, of seeking more life. Bloom is fond of quoting Rabbi Tarphon in the *Pirke Aboth:* "You are not required to complete the work, but neither are you free to desist from it." In older modes of Jewish writing, as we have seen Scholem demonstrate, this reverence for tradition, experienced as a kind of living simultaneity of all the generations, actually allows for—indeed, imposes an obligation for—further textual invention.

Modern, that is, post-Enlightenment Jewish literature is in a somewhat different situation. Speaking of Yiddish, the first Jewish language to see the birth of a truly secular literature, Irving Howe and Eliezer Greenberg observe that the Haskalah contributed "the *idea* of writing—that is, the idea that a secular career as a writer was worthy of a mature Jewish intelligence."[5] Yet since the Haskalah, Jewish writers, however secure they might be in their identities *as* writers, are still anxious about their relationship to tradition. Unlike the religious commentators of old, modern Jewish writers cannot accept the historical construction of an eternal present in which all the generations, together, as it were, at Sinai, simultaneously contribute to the unfolding of the Word. In this respect at least, modern writers' experience of rupture, of the breakages of history and tradition, is much less repressed. A work like "The Prague Orgy" is obsessed with discontinuity; its very existence as verbal form depends upon the constant awareness of rupture and loss.

Nostalgia comes into play at just this point. Nostalgia, especially for an unbroken cultural tradition, is for secular Jewish writers what the eternal present of the religious tradition was for their rabbinic forebears. In the latter instance, a literary ideology (for that, I think, is what Scholem means when he says "historical construction") of unending verbal plenitude inspires generations of devout yet frequently audacious commentators. In the former instance, under conditions which obtain from the Haskalah to the present, an ideology of loss and absence (however tempered by broad comedy or acerbic wit) enables secular authors to manipulate their relation to the past, writing out of their melancholy sense of temporal distance. Susan Sontag tells us that the saturnine Walter Benjamin "adopted a completely digested, analytical way of relating the past. It evokes events for the reactions to the events, places for the encounter with oneself, feelings and behavior for intimations of future passions and failures contained in them."[6] Something of the sort was adopted by subsequent Jewish writers as well. It may be difficult to think of nostalgic discourse as analytical, but given the conditions of exile under which modern Jewish intellectuals do their work (Benjamin's case being one of the most extreme), Sontag's formulation makes a great deal of sense. Nostalgic writers appear to give themselves to the past, but their real concern is less with the past per se than with their efforts in the present and future. Writing about the past with a controlling sense of loss and melancholy is not only a matter of analysis; it demonstrates what Benjamin calls "a tactical instinct" as well.

Because they self-consciously nurture an idealized image of the past, the authors I have discussed in this book possess, to borrow another of Benjamin's terms, "a *weak* Messianic power." As he explains:

> our image of happiness is indissolubly bound up with the image of redemption. The same applies to our view of the past, which is the concern of history. The past carries with it

a temporal index by which it is referred to redemption. There is a secret agreement between past generations and the present one. Our coming was expected on earth. Like every generation that preceded us, we have been endowed with a *weak* Messianic power, a power to which the past has a claim. That claim cannot be settled cheaply. Historical materialists are aware of that.[7]

Benjamin believed that it was the Marxist in him who gauged the present by the redemptive image of the happy past, but as is true throughout the *Theses on the Philosophy of History,* it was as much the Jew, secularized but still yearning for theological truth. In their attempt to reclaim what they have been denied, reconstitute what has been scattered, Benjamin and his literary descendants do not retreat from the present into the past but rather maintain an oppositional stance: what they perceive to be the cultural poverty or sterility of the present cannot compare to the richness, the vitality of the cherished image-world of the past; therefore it is the task of nostalgic writers to expose the present using whatever means and genres available to them. In doing so they seek to remake the present in their own image, while at the same time settling the claims of past generations.

A recent essay by Cynthia Ozick epitomizes this temporal dialectic. Ozick works harder than any other figure under consideration here at establishing links between modern writing and older Jewish traditions of textuality; she is constantly uncovering—or inventing—historical parallels between earlier and more recent linguistic circumstances, lines of influence from past to present generations. As we have seen, she is a relentless revisionist in both her criticism and her fiction. Her career-long "denial of rupture" and faith in a literary version of the Covenant are certainly signs of nostalgia, but what marks her work as a particularly refined and nuanced version of this condition is what she calls in the essay "Bialik's Hint" (1983) "the Jewish Idea." More abstract in its conception and application than any other version of nostalgia as a literary strategy, "the Jewish Idea" may well represent a turning point in the development of modern Jewish literature. And this is precisely how Ozick would have us regard her formulation.

"Bialik's Hint" revises "Toward a New Yiddish" (1970), but in doing so, it only makes Ozick's nostalgic sensibility and tactics more subtle. Looking back to her earlier work, Ozick reminds us of how she once conceived of a midrashic literature, a literature of fictive commentary written in a liturgical tongue, a Judaized English, a New Yiddish. The literature of the New Yiddish would go beyond the writing of "ethnicity," of the post-immigration experience, as best represented by Bellow, Malamud, Paley, and (presumably the early) Roth, which could not be continued without lapsing into "ventriloquism, fakery, nostalgia, sentimentalism, cardboard romanticism." The new literature would not be *ethnically* Jewish but *conceptually* Jewish, ruled by two of Ozick's by now familiar ideals: "the standard of anti-idolatry" and "the standard of distinction-making." Whereas the older literature was *local,* the new literature would be *universal:* because it was guided by enduring historical principles rather than specific sociological conditions, it would bring modern Jewish literature from the margin into the center. This new literature would reveal, as the older literature could not, that "to be a Jew is to be a member of a distinct civilization expressed through an oceanic culture in possession of a group of essential concepts and a multitude of texts and attitudes elucidating those concepts."[8] A literature of meaning, it would oppose the aestheticism and idolatry which Ozick saw in fashionable Postmodern writing.

Such was Ozick's previous theorizing. What she offers in "Bialik's Hint" is less programmatic but even more culturally ambitious. Drawing on Bialik's essay on Aggadah and Halakah (known to Benjamin as well through Scholem's German translation), Ozick argues that Bialik's dialectical understanding of these two modes emerges from his modern, post-Enlightenment mentality. The intermingling of imaginative freedom (Aggadah) and legalistic responsibility (Halakah) which Bialik expounds actually represents a fusion of Western Enlightenment ideals and the values of traditional Jewish thought. "Bialik's hint," according to Ozick, is just this fusion. Just as Judaism merged with Hellenic philosophy to produce the rabbinic idea of textual devotion, so we must now work "for Enlightenment ideas of skepticism, originality, individuality, and the assertiveness of the free imagination to leach into what we might call the Jewish language of restraint, sobriety, moral seriousness, collective conscience."[9] Once again, the Jewish Idea endures the sea-changes of history, asserting its centrality in the development of Western culture.

This is Jewish literary nostalgia on a grand scale. I have already identified Ozick's resistance to historical rupture and her insistence upon the continuity of Jewish literary traditions as constituting an authorial ideology: "the Jewish Idea" extends this formation beyond the realm of Jewish letters into the larger domain of cultural politics. Mark Krupnick has pointed out how Ozick's interest in T. S. Eliot (about whom she has recently published a long essay) is as much a matter of emulation as critique, the shtetl replacing the organic Christian society, the Jewish Idea succeeding Anglo-Catholic authority.[10] Eliot transformed Christian nostalgia into an aggressive, and for a time hegemonic modernist program. Ozick cannot expect to meet with quite the same success; besides, she is willing to fuse her Jewish cultural model with that of the Enlightenment, which Eliot utterly despised. Nevertheless, this comparison provides us with a means of judging the present state of Jewish writing, as represented by one of its major practitioners.

From the 1930s through the 1960s, ethnically Jewish writers and intellectuals dramatically changed the landscape of American culture. The Jewish-American novel redefined American fiction, and the impact of the New York intellectuals upon the field of cultural criticism was no less important. By the time Ozick arrives on the scene, these powerful influences are on the wane, and she is probably correct in her assumption that ethnic writing is a dead end. By proposing a new literary vision that is more firmly based on abstract Jewish ideas and more comprehensive in its historical perspective, Ozick believes that she can bring about a shift in the cultural values of both Jewish and non-Jewish readers to an even greater extent than did her predecessors. Writers of the older generation (novelists like Bellow and Malamud, critics like Trilling and Howe) transformed identifiably Jewish values into "moral seriousness," a cultural coin of the forties and fifties which lost a good deal of its value with the advent of high-spirited Postmodernism in the sixties. Ozick returns moral seriousness to its Jewish context but maintains its centrality for the entire culture.

Turning somewhat from her earlier position, which had revived the uncomfortable tension of the Hebraism versus Hellenism dispute, Ozick, by positing the fusion of Bialik's hint, presents herself as thoughtfully righting the balance. Without necessarily downgrading the achievements of Christianity or of the secular Englightenment, Ozick appears as a fairly liberal arbiter of culture, at least in comparison to Eliot with all his well-known prejudices. I suppose that culture must have its arbiters; indeed, their arbitrations constitute culture as a transmissible entity. Still an advocate of what Eliot calls "the main current," Ozick regrets "the diminishment of history and tradition: not to incorporate into an educable mind the origins and unifying principles of one's own civilization strikes me as a kind of cultural autolobotomy."[11] This type of rhetoric (one hears the same from Ozick's sometime sparring partner, George Steiner) reveals the compatibility of Jewish moral seriousness with the High Modernist program. Aesthetic innovation and individual expression must remain aligned with ethics, judgment, religion. Ozick cannot abide the passage of modernism; in effect she is nostalgic for a cultural moment that was in itself premised upon nostalgia: "For the modernists, the center notoriously did not hold; for us (whatever *we* are) there is no recollection of a center, and nothing to miss, let alone mourn."[12] So goes Ozick's uncanny new *kaddish*.

"Whatever *we* are": it is a troublesome *we*. Readers of *The New Yorker*? Of *Commentary*? Those who feel they have an ongoing stake in the condition of our culture? Jews who feel this way? No doubt for Ozick the answer is all of the above, and more. In Chapter One, I argued that one of Ozick's constituencies—Jewish literary intellectuals, and by extension, cultured, more or less assimilated Jews— responds with suspicion and distress to the Postmodern disintegration of the "metanarratives" which were born of the crisis of modernity. For this group, the remaking of Judaism under the auspices of modernity must remain a viable project if it is to maintain its intellectual vitality and general cultural relevance. It can neither fully return to traditional Jewish life nor can it renounce its claims to at least some of those traditions, however remade by the forces of modern history. This borderline condition keeps contemporary Jewish writers and intellectuals particularly susceptible to nostalgia.

Perhaps the susceptibility to nostalgia as both mood and strategy which I have been attempting to describe is in itself a minor metanarrative, as peculiarly related to Jewish traditions as its great cousins, psychoanalysis and Marxism. Less systematic, less given to becoming a *Weltanschauung*, this little tale which I hear reciting itself in the books of such a variety of Jewish authors provides a degree of melancholy solace in a world that is defined by the continual shock of change. At the same time, it also provides the motivating force for new work, which always appears as a product of the dialectics of revision which Jewish authors inherit and invent.

If a post-Enlightenment metanarrative of nostalgia is still at work in Jewish writing, then the passage from ethnic literature to an as yet undefined mode of writing based on "Jewish ideas" may not be as significant as the concerned reader would at first suspect. Irving

Howe, for example, regrets the end of the immigrant experience, believing that the matter of "Jewishness" "does not yield a thick enough sediment of felt life to enable a new burst of writing about American Jews."[13] It could be, ironically, that Howe's concern is less for Jewish writing than for immigrant American writing, a mode in American literature which is certainly past its prime—at least for European immigrants to America. Howe cites Ruth Wisse, who observes that recent Jewish-American writers tend to ship their characters "to other times and other climes, in search of pan-Jewish fictional atmospheres."[14] But then, why should Jewish writing be grounded in the particulars of its local place and culture? After all, the preeminent Jewish experience for thousands of years has been that of dispersal and transformation, of the creation of counterlives, to use Philip Roth's term. Not one immigration but hundreds shape the Jewish consciousness, and Jewish writers with their Aggadic sensibilities operate upon the raw material of their identities in ways which actively upset reified notions of any single, "genuine" Jewish time and place. In the terms of my argument, the nostalgia of critics like Howe and Wisse is too limited in its scope. It is tied to specific locales—the shtetl, the Lower East Side—Jewish homes, not Jewish homelessness. The adoption of writing from these milieux as the single high point in modern Jewish literature cannot be anything but sentimental, in a way that the best of this work almost never is. It is nostalgic, but strategically nostalgic, and evokes images of the past not to preserve but to disseminate them. As Howe himself says in one of his more dialectical moments, "Tradition as discontinuity—this is the central fact in the cultural experience of the American Jewish writers."[15]

Consider Saul Bellow's "The Old System," one of the finest Jewish-American tales of post-immigration life. The title presumably refers to the complex system of values, relationships, and social transactions which the Braun family has maintained, not without trial, since coming to America—"How It Was Done in Odessa," to compare it to the title of one of Babel's Jewish tales. The emphasis is precisely on the continuity of tradition we have come to regard as an ideological defense. This ostensible continuity is embodied in the figure of Isaac Braun, whose "old-country Jewish dignity was very firm and strong. He had the outlook of ancient generations on the New World. Tents and kine and wives and maidservants and manservants."[16] Isaac, whose "Orthodoxy only increased with his wealth," is challenged by his jealous, stubborn, obese sister Tina, who resents her brother and fails to help him in a shady real estate transaction with the "old goy" Ilkington. The ensuing quarrel splits the family for years, and is resolved only at Tina's deathbed, when Isaac, after consulting his *rebbe,* agrees to present his sister with $20,000 in cash, simply for the privilege of seeing her one last time. The old system of tribal debts and responsibilities is restored; the traditional code of behavior is preserved even as its bearers suffer, prosper, and live out their lives in the New World.

Surely this is a story which Bellow premises upon a strategic use of nostalgia, and in doing so he takes a bold aesthetic risk. What saves the narrative from sentimentality is the ambiguity of its values, and its troubling doubts about its own discursive authority. Seeing how the Braun family behaves, one is forced to question the exact meaning of the old system. Does it extend beyond the ethnic and family loyalties, the religious devotion, the wholehearted emotional life? Does it include the obstinacy, the greed, the venality, and the crude desires of the Brauns as well? Isaac's patriarchal world consists of the Psalms, of real estate, and of sexual adventures among the working-class women of Schenectady. His portrait is matched by that of Tina, whose gross, vital appetites, coarse speech, and defiant resolve make her an equally ambiguous character. At the heart of the old system are personalities like Isaac's and Tina's; such profane, disruptive natures are as much a part of the tradition as the continuities of family, language, and religious observance.

"The Old System" is narrated through the consciousness and memories of Dr. Braun, Isaac's and Tina's younger cousin, after the two siblings have died. Dr. Braun, a famous scientist, looks back upon this family history with deep affection, but even as he plunges into his world of memory, he observes that "every civilized man today cultivated an uneasy self-detachment." He regards this self-detachment as the necessary response to what he understands as the defining condition of contemporary life: "It made him sad to feel that the thought, art, belief of great traditions should be so misemployed."[17] Thus a subtle sense of regret and a melancholy lack of confidence informs his otherwise exuberant reminiscence.

Bellow's general cultural conservatism is certainly at work here, and that accounts in part for the nostalgic tenor of the story and its narrator. But in this instance, such gloomy mandarinism is put in the service of what Sontag calls an "analytical way of relating the past." By producing the tale through memory, Dr. Braun challenges himself, even as Bellow challenges his reader, to consider his personal and cultural values: what has been lost, what has been preserved, what will continue to be of worth. Dr. Braun's conclusion, as he thinks of Isaac reunited with Tina at her death, might be called a specimen of skeptical Jewish humanism, full of the rich emotions of the past and peering dubiously into the future:

> Oh, these Jews—these Jews! Their feelings, their hearts! Dr. Braun often wanted nothing more than to stop all this. For what came of it? One after another you gave over your dying. One by one they went. Childhood, family, friendship, love were stifled in the grave. And these tears! When you wept them from the heart, you felt you justified something, understood something. But what did you understand? Again, *nothing!* It was only an intimation of understanding. A promise that mankind might—*might,* mind you—eventually, through its gift which might—*might* again!—be a divine gift, comprehend why it lived. Why life, why death.[18]

The undeniable rhetorical triumph of this passage should not be equated with the endurance of the old system which Dr. Braun so loves and respects, unless the old system is understood to include those doubts—those italicized *mights*—about which the skeptical scientist is so emphatic. The end of Bellow's story is thus a perfect example of what Howe calls "tradition as discontinuity." The old system continually undergoes change, and it consists in part of the disruption and doubt through which it is reinvigorated. In this respect, Bellow's warmly local ethnic writing achieves its ends in much the same way as the expansive pronouncements of Ozick or the artful mirror games of Roth—or for that matter, the theorizing of Benjamin and Scholem, the original masters of modern Jewish nostalgia.

Nostalgia as an ensemble of literary strategies or as a psychohistorical metanarrative is closely linked to the wandering meanings and textual homelands I have analyzed throughout this book. The Jews, we are told, are as at home in time as other peoples are in space; the various ideologies of exile have not only eased our worldly burdens, teaching us to accept and even rejoice in our spatial wanderings, but have acclimated us to the irreversible order of time, what Olivier Revault d'Allonnes calls "the sole reality on which one can count." Jewish writers, acutely sensitive to the nuanced movements of time, look back to earlier moments, often encoded in earlier texts; after all, "the flashback does not exist in reality: one can return to the past only by narrative or by phantasm."[19] The nostalgic consciousness and the textual homeland are complements for Jewish writers, together forming a basic literary economy: the strategies of nostalgia, when best put to use, achieve a place—no, a time—of fullness, a temporary victory to which later writers will look back in turn. The finest practitioners of this melancholy art seem capable of bridging vast spaces of time, filling empty years with strange presences, phantasms which are and are not, as in these moving lines from John Hollander's recent "Marks and Noises":

> Long afterwards, abandoned alphabets
> Which could not stand for language any more
> The disused runes, the dark, square Hebrew letters
> Adrift in Christendom, shriveled to mere
> Magic, and long since silenced hieroglyphs
> Faded into pictures of mysteries.
> O letters! O domestic ghosts! the spectres
> Of dead speech, they rise up about me now
> From stillborn sounds laid out on this lined sheet.[20]

This new work is as full of diasporic nostalgia as any of the others I have considered here. I find it strange then that Harold Bloom, who naturally sees his friend Hollander as one of the best Jewish-American poets, and who has served as one of the most important guides in my own textual wandering, should now tell us that Jews in America are no longer in exile. For as Bloom observes in "Jewish Culture and Jewish Identity, "The old formulae of *Galut* simply do not work in the diffuse cultural contexts of America."[21] Nevertheless, Jewish-American writers and intellectuals still must look back to such figures as Freud and Kafka because "The absence of overwhelming cultural achievement compels us to rely upon the cultural identity of the last phases of the *Galut*, yet we, as I have said before, scarcely feel that we are in Exile."[22]

It is an oddly cheerful opinion, but then, Bloom's prophecies have never been consistent; and I, for one, am not yet ready to agree with this one. Sociologically speaking, Jews may well feel as at home as any other American minority (and we are by now a nation of minorities), but sociology, whatever tools it may provide for the literary critic, can never fully account for the vicissitudes of literary creation. If, as Bloom himself notes, a Jewish-American writer like Philip Roth still resorts to the wandering meanings of Kafka and

Freud, then Jewish-American *culture* is still a culture of exile, and I see little reason to either hope for or to expect a change.

Once again, Nathan Zuckerman comes to mind, this time in *The Counterlife*. Having faced the lunacy of his brother's conversion to right-wing Zionism in Israel and the ugliness of his in-laws' anti-Semitism in England, Zuckerman is urging Maria, his pregnant wife, to return to him. If their child turns out to be a boy, he wants to have a *bris*, because

> Circumcision makes it clear as can be that you are here and not there, that you are out and not in—also that you're mine and not theirs. There is no way around it: you enter history through my history and me. Circumcision is everything that the pastoral is not and, to my mind, reinforces what the world is about, which isn't strifeless unity. Quite convincingly, circumcision gives the lie to the womb-dream of life in the beautiful state of innocent prehistory, the appealing idyll of living "naturally," unencumbered by man-made ritual. To be born is to lose all that. The heavy hand of human values falls upon you right at the start, marking your genitals as its own. Inasmuch as one invents one's meanings, along with impersonating one's selves, this is the meaning I propose for that rite.[23]

This is genuine modern midrash, as clear an example of the ritual of new creation as I can offer. Compelled to meditate upon the ancient rite, Zuckerman finds new meaning that is commensurate with the circumstances of his ceaselessly destabilized existence. As he observes from the vantage point in the home of the pastoral,

> Circumcision confirms that there is an us, and an us that isn't solely him and me. England's made a Jew of me in only eight weeks, which, on reflection, might be the least painful method. A Jew without Jews, without Judaism, without Zionism, without Jewishness, without a temple or an army or even a pistol, a Jew clearly without a home, just the object itself, like a glass or an apple.[24]

I am not at all sure that I understand what Roth, after such an immersion in history and tradition, really means by a Jew who is "just the object itself," but I still find this passage immensely appealing. It may well serve as a model for Jewish literature for some time to come.

NOTES

Introduction

1. Harold Bloom, "Introduction," *Musical Variations On Jewish Thought,* by Olivier Revault D'Allonnes (New York: George Braziller, 1984), 30.

2. Harold Bloom, *Agon: Towards a Theory of Revisionism* (New York: Oxford University Press, 1982), 320.

3. Gershom Scholem, "Revelation and Tradition as Religious Categories in Judaism," in *The Messianic Idea in Judaism* (New York: Schocken Books, 1971), 289.

4. Edmond Jabès, "The Key," in *Midrash and Literature,* ed. by Geoffrey H. Hartman and Sandford Budick (New Haven: Yale University Press, 1986), 352.

5. Walter Benjamin, *Illuminations,* trans. Harry Zohn (New York: Schocken Books, 1968), 139.

6. Gershom Scholem, *On the Kabbalah and Its Symbolism,* trans. Ralph Manheim (New York: Schocken Books, 1965), 126.

7. Yosef Hayim Yerushalmi, *Zakhor: Jewish History and Jewish Memory* (Seattle: University of Washington Press, 1982), 101.

8. *The Diaries of Franz Kafka: 1914–1923,* ed. Max Brod, trans. Martin Greenberg (New York: Schocken Books, 1949), 202–203.

9. Harold Bloom, *Ruin the Sacred Truths: Poetry and Belief from the Bible to the Present* (Cambridge: Harvard University Press, 1989), 172.

10. Ibid., 4.

11. George Steiner, *Real Presences* (Chicago: University of Chicago Press, 1989), 4.

12. Ibid., 134.

13. George Steiner, "Our Homeland, the Text," *Salmagundi* No. 66 (Winter–Spring 1985): 9–10.

14. Cynthia Ozick, *Art and Ardor* (New York: Knopf, 1983), 169.

15. Cf. Henry Louis Gates, Jr., *The Signifying Monkey: A Theory of African-American Literary Criticism* (New York: Oxford University Press, 1988), 237: "In literature, blackness is produced in the text only through a complex process of signification. There can be no transcendental blackness, for it cannot and does not exist beyond manifestations of it in specific figures." Gates's critique of cultural essences, as in the notion of "transcendental blackness," and his emphasis instead on the linguistically produced or constructed ("signifying") quality of an identifiably "ethnic" writing, makes his work very useful in any debate over what makes a book "black," "Jewish," etc.

16. Bloom, "Introduction," 6.

17. Jabès, "The Key," 352.

18. Ibid., 353–54.

19. Jacques Derrida, *Writing and Difference,* trans. Alan Bass (Chicago: University of Chicago Press, 1978), 297.

20. See, for example, Robert Alter, "Old Rabbis, New Critics," *The New Republic,* January 5 & 12, 1987, 27–33; David Stern, "Midrash and Indeterminacy," *Critical Inquiry* 15 (Autumn 1988): 132–161.

21. Stern, "Midrash and Indeterminacy," 161.

22. Regarding the relationship of ideology to the utopian and the messianic, see Norman Finkelstein, "The Utopian Function and the Refunctioning of Marxism," *Diacritics* 19 No. 2 (1989): 54–65; and *The Utopian Moment in Contemporary American Poetry* (Lewisburg, PA: Bucknell University Press, 1988), 13–28.

23. Scholem, *The Messianic Idea,* 35.

24. Derrida, *Writing and Difference,* 292.

25. Allen Mandelbaum, *Chelmaxioms* (Boston: David R. Godine, 1977), 15.

26. Benjamin, *Illuminations,* 145.

Chapter 1. Postmodernism and the Jewish Literary Intellectual

1. Isaac Deutscher, *The Non-Jewish Jew and Other Essays* (New York: Oxford University Press, 1968), 26.

2. Ibid., 35. For an interpretation of the figure of the non-Jewish Jew, especially in relation to American life, see Mark Shechner, *After the Revolution: Studies in the Contemporary Jewish American Imagination* (Bloomington: Indiana University Press, 1987), 12–13, 240–242.

3. Fredric Jameson, "Postmodernism, or The Cultural Logic of Late Capitalism," *New Left Review* 146 (July–August 1984): 66.

4. Benjamin, *Illuminations,* 255.

5. See Ozick, *Art and Ardor,* 155–177, 238–248; Marshall Berman, *All That Is Solid Melts Into Air: The Experience of Modernity* (New York: Penguin, 1988), 9–10, and "Why Modernism Still Matters," *Tikkun* 4, No. 1 (January/February 1989): 82–84.

6. Revault D'Allonnes, *Musical Variations On Jewish Thought,* 77.

7. Saul Friedlander, *Reflections of Nazism: An Essay on Kitsch and Death,* trans. Thomas Weyr (New York: Harper & Row, 1984), *passim.*

8. Jameson, "Postmodernism," 66.

9. Jean-Francois Lyotard, *The Post-Modern Condition: A Report on Knowledge,* trans. Geoff Bennington & Brian Massumi (Minneapolis: University of Minnesota Press, 1984), xxiv.

10. Lionel Trilling, *Beyond Culture: Essays on Literature and Learning* (New York: Viking, 1968), 184.

11. Franz Kafka, "Letter to His Father," trans. Richard and Clara Winston, in *The Basic Kafka* (New York: Washington Square Press, 1979), 216.

12. John Murray Cuddihy, *The Ordeal of Civility: Freud, Marx, Levi-Strauss, and the Jewish Struggle With Modernity* (New York: Basic Books, 1974), 38.

13. Ibid., 40.

14. Jameson, "Postmodernism," 63.

15. Ibid., 64.

16. Benjamin, *Illuminations,* 221.

17. Jacques Derrida, *Margins of Philosophy,* trans. Alan Bass (Chicago: University of Chicago Press, 1982), 21–22.

18. Ibid., 11.

19. Shechner, *After the Revolution,* 8.

20. Mark Krupnick, *Lionel Trilling and the Fate of Cultural Criticism,* (Evanston, IL: Northwestern University Press, 1986), 1–18.

21. Diana Trilling, "Lionel Trilling: A Jew at Columbia," in Lionel Trilling, *Speaking of Literature,* ed. Diana Trilling (New York: Harcourt Brace Jovanovich, 1980), 422.

22. Sidney Hook, "Anti-Semitism in the Academy: Some Pages of the Past," *Midstream* 25 (January 1979): 51–53.

23. Alfred Kazin, *New York Jew* (New York: Knopf, 1978), 43.

24. Diana Trilling, "Lionel Trilling," 413.

25. Lionel Trilling, *The Liberal Imagination: Essays on Literature and Society* (New York: Viking, 1950), 206–207. One cannot quote from this essay without also noting Delmore Schwartz's devastating (and hilarious) critique, "The Duchess' Red Shoes." According to Schwartz, Trilling is not truly concerned with literature per se, but with "the ideas and attitudes and interests of the educated class, such as it is and such as it may become: it is of this class that he is, at heart, the guardian and critic." Thus Trilling misleadingly uses literary criticism as a medium for social criticism, and vice versa. More recent critics might argue that Schwartz is setting up a false dichotomy, but I still agree with his basic insight: to a great extent, Trilling is a social commentator in the guise of a literary critic. Arguably, it is a late version of "the ordeal of civility" that transformed him into such a figure. See *Selected Essays of Delmore Schwartz,* ed. David A. Dike & David. H. Zucker (Chicago: University of Chicago Press, 1985), 212.

26. Lionel Trilling, *Sincerity and Authenticity* (Cambridge: Harvard University Press, 1972), 172.

27. Lionel Trilling, *The Opposing Self: Nine Essays in Criticism* (New York: Viking, 1955), 128.

28. Ibid., 131.

29. Ibid., 143.

30. Schechner, *After the Revolution,* 57.

31. Bloom, *Ruin the Sacred Truths,* 4.

32. Ibid., 161.

33. Ibid., 168.

34. Ibid., 154.

35. Trilling, *The Liberal Imagination,* 53.

36. Bloom, *Agon,* 39.

37. Quoted in Imre Salusinszky, *Criticism in Society* (New York: Methuen, 1987), 73.

38. Harold Bloom, *Kabbalah and Criticism* (New York: Continuum, 1984), 90.

39. Bloom, *Ruin the Sacred Truths,* 179.

40. Bloom, *Agon,* 322.

41. Charles Newman, *The Post-Modern Aura: The Act of Fiction in an Age of Inflation* (Evanston, IL: Northwestern University Press, 1985), 16.

Chapter 2. Harold Bloom; Or, the Sage of New Haven

1. Harold Bloom, *The Anxiety of Influence: A Theory of Poetry* (New York: Oxford University Press, 1973), 95.

2. Bloom, *Agon,* 19.

3. Harold Bloom, *The Breaking of the Vessels* (Chicago: University of Chicago Press, 1982), 3.

4. Bloom, *Agon,* 39.

5. Jean-Pierre Mileur, *Literary Revisionism and the Burden of Modernity* (Berkeley: University of California Press, 1985), 58–59.

6. Harold Bloom, *A Map of Misreading* (New York: Oxford University Press, 1975), 29.

7. Bloom, *Breaking of the Vessels,* 38.

8. Bloom, *Map of Misreading,* 29.

9. Bloom, *Breaking of the Vessels,* 3.

10. Bloom, *Map of Misreading,* 60.

11. Bloom, *Agon,* 39.

12. Ibid., 39.

13. Ibid., 12.

14. Bloom, *Kabbalah and Criticism,* 90.

15. Ibid., 63–64.

16. Frank Lentricchia, *After the New Criticism* (Chicago: University of Chicago Press, 1980), 338.

17. Bloom, *Kabbalah and Criticism,* 85–86.

18. Ibid., 126.

19. *Selections from Ralph Waldo Emerson,* ed. Stephen E. Whicher (Boston: Houghton Mifflin, 1957), 376.

20. Bloom, *Map of Misreading*, 39.

21. Bloom, *Agon*, 18.

22. Bloom, *Breaking of the Vessels*, 26.

23. Emerson, *Selections*, 225.

24. Mileur, *Literary Revisionism*, 57.

25. Ibid., 75.

26. Bloom, *Map of Misreading*, 29.

27. Ibid., 38.

28. Bloom, *Breaking of the Vessels*, 29.

29. Mileur, *Literary Revisionism*, 18.

30. Bloom, *Breaking of the Vessels*, 70.

31. Mileur, *Literary Revisionism*, 65–66.

32. Michel Foucault, "What is Enlightenment?," in *The Foucault Reader,* ed. Paul Rabinow (New York: Pantheon, 1984), 45–46.

33. Bloom, *Agon*, 31.

34. Bloom, *Anxiety of Influence*, 85–86.

35. Ibid., 9.

36. Sigmund Freud, *Civilization and Its Discontents,* trans. James Strachey (New York: Norton, 1961), 75.

37. Bloom, *Anxiety of Influence*, 25.

38. Bloom, *Map of Misreading*, 42–43.

39. Bloom, *Breaking of the Vessels*, 4.

40. Bloom, *Kabbalah and Criticism*, 40.

41. Bloom, *Map of Misreading*, 61.

42. Ibid., 32.

43. Bloom, *Kabbalah and Criticism*, 98, 100.

44. Ibid., 103.

45. Bloom, *Agon*, 285.

46. Scholem, *The Messianic Idea in Judaism*, 284.

47. Gerald L. Bruns, "Canon and Power in the Hebrew Scriptures," in *Canons,* ed. Robert Von Hallberg (Chicago: University of Chicago Press, 1984), 67.

48. Bloom, *Kabbalah and Criticism,* 52.

49. Bloom, "Introduction," 29.

50. Robert Moynihan, "Interview: Harold Bloom," *Diacritics* (Fall 1983): 67.

51. Gershom Scholem, *On Jews and Judaism In Crisis* (New York: Schocken Books, 1978), 262.

52. David Biale, *Gershom Scholem: Kabbalah and Counter-History* (Cambridge: Harvard University Press, 1979), 111.

53. Bloom, "Introduction," 7.

54. Bloom, *Kabbalah and Criticism,* 82–83.

55. Scholem, *The Messianic Idea in Judaism,* 284–289.

56. Bloom, *Breaking of the Vessels,* 52.

57. Ozick, *Art and Ardor,* 199.

58. Bloom, *Kabbalah and Criticism,* 47.

59. Mileur, *Literary Revisionism,* 56–57.

60. Biale, *Gershom Scholem,* 191. For another discussion of Bloom, Scholem and Biale, see Susan A. Handelman, *The Slayers of Moses: The Emergence of Rabbinic Interpretation in Modern Literary Theory* (Albany: SUNY Press, 1982), 197–208. For Handelman, the revisionism of Scholem and Bloom (and of other Jewish thinkers such as Freud and Derrida) places them both inside and outside the tradition, a contradictory placement which has become the sine qua non of the tradition as it has been passed down and transformed in the modern period. We can only know tradition through revisionism—but according to Scholem and Bloom, it is only through revision that the tradition has ever known itself.

61. Bloom, *Map of Misreading,* 42.

62. Barry W. Holtz, "Midrash," in *Back to the Sources: Reading the Classic Jewish Texts,* ed. Barry W. Holtz (New York: Summit Books, 1984), 181.

63. Bloom, "Introduction," 9–10.

64. James L. Kugel, "Two Introductions to Midrash," in *Midrash and Literature,* ed. Geoffrey H. Hartman and Sanford Budick (New Haven: Yale University Press, 1986), 92.

65. Ibid., 93.

66. Bloom, *Kabbalah and Criticism,* 33.

67. Arthur Green, *Tormented Master: A Life of Rabbi Nahman of Bratslav* (University of Alabama Press, 1979; New York: Schocken Books, 1981), 287.

68. Mileur, *Literary Revisionism,* 110.

Chapter 3. Gershom Scholem and Literary Criticism

1. Ozick, *Art and Ardor,* 138–139.

2. Joseph Dan, *Gershom Scholem and the Mystical Dimension of Jewish History* (New York: New York University Press, 1987), 27–28.

3. Derrida, *Writing and Difference,* 292.

4. Gershom Scholem, *Kabbalah* (New York: New American Library, 1974), 111–112.

5. Derrida, *Writing and Difference,* 293.

6. Robert Alter, *Defenses of the Imagination: Jewish Writers and Modern Historical Crisis* (Philadelphia: Jewish Publication Society of America, 1977), 81.

7. Ibid., 82.

8. Frank Lentricchia, "Series Editor's Forward," in *The Breaking of the Vessels,* by Harold Bloom (Chicago: University of Chicago Press, 1982), x.

9. Bloom, *Kabbalah and Criticism,* 17–18.

10. Ozick, *Art and Ardor,* 147.

11. Scholem, *On the Kabbalah,* 9.

12. Ibid., 11.

13. Scholem, *The Messianic Idea in Judaism,* 285–286.

14. Ibid., 289.

15. Ibid., 288.

16. Ibid., 295.

17. Ibid., 296.

18. Scholem, *On the Kabbalah,* 49–50.

19. Ibid., 21.

20. Quoted in Biale, *Gershom Scholem,* 75.

21. Anson Rabinbach, "Introduction," in *The Correspondence of Walter Benjamin and Gershom Scholem 1932–1940,* trans. Gary Smith and Andre Lefevere (New York: Schocken Books, 1989), xxxii.

22. Ibid., 127.

23. Ibid., xxxii.

24. Franz Kafka, *Letters to Friends, Family and Editors,* trans. Richard and Clara Winston (New York: Schocken Books, 1977), 282.

25. Wallace Stevens, *The Collected Poems of Wallace Stevens* (New York: Knopf, 1954), 417.

26. Ibid., 423–424.

27. Harold Bloom, *Wallace Stevens: The Poems of Our Climate* (Ithaca: Cornell University Press, 1977), 89.

28. Stevens, *Collected Poems,* 18.

29. Ibid., 389.

30. Ibid., 420.

31. Ibid., 325.

32. Scholem, *On the Kabbalah,* 124.

33. Bloom, *Kabbalah and Criticism,* 88.

34. Stevens, *Collected Poems,* 524.

35. Scholem, *On the Kabbalah,* 7. Cf. the last lines of Scholem's anthology of readings from the *Zohar:* "Just as wine must be in a jar to keep, so the Torah must be contained in an outer garment. That garment is made up of the tales and stories; but we, we are bound to penetrate beyond." *Zohar: The Book of Splendor,* ed. Gershom Scholem (New York: Schocken Books, 1949), 122.

36. Scholem, *On Jews and Judaism in Crisis,* 46.

37. Terry Eagleton, *Walter Benjamin or Towards a Revolutionary Criticism* (London: Verso, 1981), 48.

Chapter 4. The Struggle for Historicity: Cynthia Ozick's Fiction

1. Yerushalmi, *Zakhor,* 98.

2. Ozick, *Art and Ardor,* 169.

3. Ibid., 248.

4. Scholem, *The Messianic Idea in Judaism,* 1.

5. Walter Benjamin, *Reflections,* trans. Edmund Jephcott (New York: Harcourt Brace Jovanovich, 1978; rpt. New York: Schocken Books, 1986), 312.

6. Ibid.

7. Benjamin, *Illuminations,* 255.

8. Ozick, *Art and Ardor,* 247.

9. Cynthia Ozick, *The Pagan Rabbi and Other Stories* (New York: Alfred A. Knopf, 1971; rpt. New York: E. P. Dutton, 1983), 42.

10. Ibid., 96.

11. Ibid.

12. Ozick, *Art and Ardor,* 247.

13. Barry W. Holtz succinctly defines and contrasts Halakhah and Aggadah: the former "refers to Jewish literature primarily concerned with law and codes of behavior," while the latter "is a looser and more wide-ranging term referring to narrative literature, parables, theological or ethical statements, and homilies.... It is, one might say, a kind of 'imaginative' literature." Holtz, "Midrash," 178. For more thorough discussions of Aggadah, see Joseph Heinemann, "The Nature of the Aggadah," and Judah Goldin, "The Freedom and Restraint of Haggadah," in *Midrash and Literature,* ed. Geoffrey H. Hartman and Sanford Budick (New Haven: Yale University Press, 1986), 41–55, 57–76.

14. Benjamin, *Illuminations,* 143–144.

15. Goldin, "The Freedom and Restraint of Haggadah," 69.

16. Tom Teicholz, "The Art of Fiction XCV: Cynthia Ozick," *Paris Review* 102 (1987): 167.

17. Harold Bloom, "Introduction," *Cynthia Ozick,* ed. Harold Bloom (New York: Chelsea House, 1986), 1.

18. Ozick, *Art and Ardor,* 246.

19. Cynthia Ozick, *Levitation: Five Fictions* (New York: Alfred A. Knopf, 1982; rpt. New York: E. P. Dutton, 1983), 120.

20. Ibid., 156.

21. For Scholes, *interpretation* "can be the result of either some excess of meaning in a text or of some deficiency in the reader," as opposed to *reading,* when all the codes in the text are accessible or negotiable. *Criti-*

cism, Scholes' third category, "involves a critique of the themes developed in a given fictional text, or a critique of the codes themselves, out of which a given text has been constructed." *Textual Power: Literary Theory and the Teaching of English* (New Haven: Yale University Press, 1985), 22, 23.

22. See Bloom's discussions of Jacob's wrestling with the angel in *The Breaking of the Vessels* (49–60) and in the "Introduction" to *Musical Variations on Jewish Thought* (12–13). For Bloom, the struggle for the Blessing "in every sense primarily means *more life*" (*Musical Variations* 27), which would come from the triumphant seizing of unbounded time from God, or more precisely from the angel, whom Bloom understands to be the Angel of Death. This sheds further light on the tragicomic defeat found throughout Ozick's work: even compared to the self-lacerating struggles in Kafka, it implies an acceptance of the contemporary Jew's diminished status within normative belief.

23. Scholes, *Textual Power,* 22.

24. Ozick, *Art and Ardor,* 208.

25. Yerushalmi, *Zakhor,* 11.

26. Ibid., 14–15.

27. Ibid., 21, 18.

28. For discussions of the significance of this movement, see Yerushalmi, *Zakhor,* 83–90 and Biale, *Gershom Scholem,* 4–32.

29. Yerushalmi, *Zakhor,* 93.

30. Bloom, "Introduction," *Musical Variations,* 11.

31. Cynthia Ozick, *The Cannibal Galaxy* (New York: Alfred A. Knopf, 1983; rpt. New York: E. P. Dutton, 1984), 5.

32. Ibid., 27.

33. Sanford Pinsker, *The Uncompromising Fiction of Cynthia Ozick* (Columbia, MO: University of Missouri Press, 1987), 105.

34. Yerushalmi, *Zakhor,* 84.

35. Ozick, *The Cannibal Galaxy,* 101.

36. Ibid., 162.

37. Ozick, *Art and Ardor,* 246.

38. Cynthia Ozick, *The Messiah of Stockholm* (New York: Alfred A. Knopf, 1987), 128.

39. Bloom, "Introduction," *Cynthia Ozick,* 7.

Chapter 5. Lost and Found:
Hollander, Mandelbaum, and the Poetry of Exile

1. Holtz, "Midrash," 179.

2. Isaac Bashevis Singer, *The Collected Stories* (New York: Farrar Straus Giroux, 1982), 14.

3. George Steiner, "North of the Future," *The New Yorker* (August 28, 1989): 95.

4. *Poems of Paul Celan,* trans. Michael Hamburger (New York: Persea Books, 1988), 161.

5. John Hollander, *Spectral Emanations: New and Selected Poems* (New York: Atheneum, 1978), 37. Subsequent references appear in the text.

6. Harold Bloom, *Figures of Capable Imagination* (New York: Seabury Press, 1976), 254.

7. Bloom, *Agon,* 307.

8. Mandelbaum, *Chelmaxioms,* xvi. Subsequent references appear in the text.

9. Bloom, *Agon,* 313.

10. Stevens, *Collected Poems,* 17.

11. See Hans Robert Jauss, *Toward an Aesthetic of Reception,* trans. Timothy Bahti (Minneapolis: University of Minnesota Press, 1982). According to Jauss,

> If one characterizes as aesthetic distance the disparity between the given horizon of expectations and the appearance of a new work, whose reception can result in a "change of horizons" through negation of familiar experiences or through raising newly articulated experiences to the level of consciousness, then this aesthetic distance can be objectified historically along the spectrum of the audience's reactions and criticism's judgment (the spontaneous success, rejection or shock, scattered approval, gradual or belated understanding.) (25)

12. Scholem, *On Jews and Judaism In Crisis,* 238.

13. Irving Howe and Eliezer Greenberg, ed., *A Treasury of Yiddish Stories* (New York: Schocken Books, 1954), 610.

14. Steiner, "Our Homeland, the Text," 25–26.

15. Ibid., 17.

16. See Scholem, *On the Kabbalah,* 137–153.

17. Scholem, *The Messianic Idea in Judaism,* 294.

18. Bloom, "Introduction," *Musical Variations,* 7.

19. Bloom, *Agon,* 291.

Chapter 6. Judaism and the Rhetoric of Authority: George Steiner's Textual Homeland

1. *George Steiner: A Reader* (New York: Oxford University Press, 1984), 20–21.

2. Franz Kafka, *The Basic Kafka,* 185.

3. George Steiner, *In Bluebeard's Castle: Some Notes Towards the Redefinition of Culture* (New Haven: Yale University Press, 1971), 81.

4. George Steiner, *Language and Silence: Essays on Language, Literature and the Inhuman* (New York: Atheneum, 1967), 34.

5. Steiner, *Real Presences,* 93.

6. Steiner, *In Bluebeard's Castle,* 68.

7. Martin Jay, *Adorno* (Cambridge: Harvard University Press, 1984), 17.

8. Steiner, *A Reader,* 13.

9. Benjamin, *Reflections,* 302.

10. Steiner, *Bluebeard's Castle,* 141.

11. Steiner, *Language and Silence,* 381.

12. Steiner, *Real Presences,* 40.

13. Steiner, "Our Homeland, the Text," 5.

14. Steiner, *Language and Silence,* 152.

15. Steiner, "Our Homeland, the Text," 21.

16. Cf. Revault d'Allonnes in *Musical Variations On Jewish Thought:* "Western anti-Semitism, in rejecting the Jew as 'different', perceived at the same time the nomadic character of Judaism and its indifference, even its hostility, to nations and to states" (51). Like Steiner, Revault d'Allonnes believes that genuine Judaism (or at least the most culturally significant form of Judaism) is nomadic; this is why, in his consideration of biblical Judaism, he favors the nomadic form of worship (the Ark carried from place to place) as opposed to the sedentary cult (the Ark enclosed in the Temple).

17. George Steiner, "A P.S.," *Salmagundi* No. 50–51 (Fall 1980–Winter 1981): 252. This comment appears in the afterword to a symposium based on "The Archives of Eden" (57–89), a essay in which Steiner argues that the United States is essentially a "museum culture" which preserves but is incapable of producing the highest types of art and thought. For Steiner, American democratic and capitalistic principles are antithetical to the creative energies required of such production, energies which are born in profound social isolation and may actually be encouraged by conditions of political repression. Thus to endorse both high culture and democratic ideals amounts to the "puerile hypocrisy and opportunism" (87) demonstrated by many American intellectuals. The essay is a good example of Steiner's elitism, which itself becomes a vulgar and all-too-easy epithet for the serious thinker engaged with problems of cultural value. "I asked myself whether my entire schooling and the intellectual and formal values which it embodied had not made the cry in the poem, the desolation in the sonata, come to seem more real, more immediate to my imaginings, than the cry in the street" (*A Reader*, 11). The writer of this sentence may well believe in the importance of a cultural elite, but also understands that one can never take the moral validity of such an elite for granted.

18. Steiner, "Our Homeland, the Text," 21.

19. Ibid., 19.

20. Ibid., 22.

21. Ibid., 23. "Our Homeland, the Text," which I consider to be one of Steiner's crucial essays, produced a revealing controversy, as have a number of Steiner's polemical pieces over the course of his career. In his attack on the essay, Lionel Abel insists on just the either/or situation for modern Judaism which Steiner is trying to circumvent: *either* secular Zionism *or* Orthodoxy. Abel is appalled by Steiner's use of the term *text,* associating it with a grotesque parody of deconstruction. What he fails to see are the strong links between traditional Jewish attitudes toward reading and writing and the modern "nomadic" stance which Steiner describes. Abel's position on Israel seems to be totally uncritical, an example of the "sleep of reason" which Steiner justly denounces. See Lionel Abel, "So Who Is to Have the Last Word? (On Some of the Positions Taken by George Steiner)," *Partisan Review* No. 3 (1986): 359–371.

22. Anson Rabinbach, "Between Enlightenment and Apocalypse: Benjamin, Bloch and Modern German Jewish Messianism," *New German Critique* 34 (Winter 1985): 81.

23. Steiner, *In Bluebeard's Castle,* 140.

24. Rabinbach, "Between Enlightenment and Apocalypse," 123.

25. Steiner, *Real Presences,* 232.

26. Steiner, *In Bluebeard's Castle*, 89.

27. Steiner, *Real Presences*, 201.

28. Ibid., 138.

29. Ibid., 86.

30. Ibid., 132.

31. Derrida, *Writing and Difference*, 293.

32. Steiner, *Language and Silence*, 10.

33. George Steiner, *The Portage to San Cristobal of A. H.* (New York: Simon and Schuster, 1981), 116.

34. Steiner, *In Bluebeard's Castle*, 23.

35. Alvin H. Rosenfeld, *Imagining Hitler* (Bloomington, IN: Indiana University Press, 1985), 98.

36. Steiner, *Language and Silence*, 163.

37. Steiner, *In Bluebeard's Castle*, 30–31.

38. Ibid., 38.

39. Ibid., 44.

40. Ibid., 45. Steiner's view of Judaism as the source of Western culture's superego is implicitly refuted in one of the funniest scenes in Philip Roth's *The Counterlife*. For the violent but crudely eloquent Israeli agent who foils Jimmy Ben-Joseph's attempt to hijack the El Al flight, anti-Semitism is to be understood in exactly the opposite terms as Steiner's analysis. As he declares to the hapless Nathan Zuckerman: "You think it's the Jewish superego they hate? *They hate the Jewish id!*" And just as Steiner revises T. S. Eliot's *Notes towards the Definition of Culture* in *In Bluebeard's Castle*, Roth revises Eliot's poetry. In the agent's diatribe, the anti-Semitic portrait of Bleistein in Eliot's poem ironically becomes a heroic symbol, "A powerful Jew with a Jewish id, smoking his big fat cigar! *Real Jewish might!* See Philip Roth, *The Counterlife* (New York: Farrar, Straus & Giroux, 1986), 178, 181.

41. Ibid., 46.

42. Rabinbach, "Between Enlightenment and Apocalypse," 86.

43. Rosenfeld, *Imagining Hitler*, 99. See also S. Lillian Kremer, *Witness Through the Imagination: Jewish American Holocaust Literature* (Detroit: Wayne State University Press, 1989), 349–355.

44. Robert Boyers, *Atrocity and Amnesia: The Political Novel Since 1945* (New York: Oxford University Press, 1985), 158. Boyers makes his point in a refutation of Hyam Maccoby's attack on *The Portage*, but what he

says applies at least to some extent to nearly everyone who has written about the work, including Rosenfeld, with whose reading Boyers mostly sympathizes. See Hyam Maccoby, "George Steiner's Hitler," *Encounter* (May 1982): 27–34.

45. Steiner, *The Portage to San Cristobal of A. H.,* 166–167.

46. Boyers, *Atrocity and Amnesia,* 170.

47. Terry Eagleton, *Marxism and Literary Criticism* (Berkeley: University of California Press, 1976), 18.

48. Steiner, *The Portage to San Cristobal of A. H.,* 169.

49. Friedlander, *Reflections of Nazism,* 2.

50. Ibid., 69–70.

51. Joseph Lowin, "Steiner's Helicopters," *Jewish Book Annual* 41 (1983–1984): 56.

52. I am indebted to Joseph Lowin for this information.

Chapter 7. Walter Benjamin, Messianism, and Marxism: A Midrash

1. Adin Steinsaltz, *The Thirteen Petalled Rose,* trans. Yehuda Hanegbi (New York: Basic Books, 1980), 54.

2. Benjamin, *Reflections,* 192.

3. Rolf Tiedemann, "Historical Materialism or Political Messianism? An Interpretation of the Theses 'On the Concept of History'," *Benjamin: Philosophy, Aesthetics, History,* ed. Gary Smith (Chicago: University of Chicago Press, 1989), 191–192.

4. Richard Wolin, *Walter Benjamin: An Aesthetic of Redemption* (New York: Columbia University Press, 1982), 205.

5. Walter Benjamin, "N [Re The Theory of Knowledge, Theory of Progress]," trans. Leigh Hafrey and Richard Sieburth, *Benjamin,* 64.

6. Scholem, *Messianic Idea in Judaism,* 35.

7. Jacob Neusner, *Messiah in Context: Israel's History and Destiny in Formative Judaism* (Philadelphia: Fortress Press, 1984), 227.

8. Cuddihy, *Ordeal of Civility,* 5.

9. Jurgen Habermas, *Philosophical-Political Profiles,* trans. Frederick G. Lawrence (Cambridge: The MIT Press, 1983), 208.

10. Wolin, *Walter Benjamin*, 182.

11. Terry Eagleton, *Walter Benjamin*, 141–142.

12. Ibid., 117.

13. Benjamin, *Reflections*, 301.

14. Benjamin, "N," 64.

Chapter 8. Nostalgia and Futurity: Jewish Literature in Transition

1. Philip Roth, *Zuckerman Bound: A Trilogy and Epilogue* (New York: Farrar Straus Giroux, 1985), 760–761.

2. Scholem, *The Messianic Idea in Judaism*, 288. See the discussion of this concept in Chapter 3.

3. Roth, *Zuckerman Bound*, 719.

4. Ibid., 767.

5. Howe and Greenberg, *Treasury of Yiddish Stories*, 25.

6. Susan Sontag, *Under the Sign of Saturn* (New York: Farrar Straus Giroux, 1980), 115.

7. Benjamin, *Illuminations*, 254.

8. Cynthia Ozick, *Metaphor and Memory* (New York: Alfred A. Knopf, 1989), 224.

9. Ibid., 237.

10. Mark Krupnick, "Cynthia Ozick as the Jewish T. S. Eliot." Paper read to the NEH summer seminar on Jewish American writing, University of Illinois, Chicago, July, 1990.

11. Cynthia Ozick, "T. S. Eliot at 101," *The New Yorker* (Nov. 20, 1989): 124.

12. Ibid., 153.

13. Irving Howe, "Introduction," *Jewish American Stories*, ed. Irving Howe (New York: New American Library, 1977), 16.

14. Ibid.

15. Ibid., 13.

16. Saul Bellow, *Mosby's Memoirs and Other Stories* (New York: Viking Press, 1968), 54.

17. Ibid., 52.

18. Ibid., 90–91.

19. Revault D'Allonnes, *Musical Variations,* 45.

20. John Hollander, *Harp Lake* (New York: Alfred A. Knopf, 1988), 28.

21. Harold Bloom, *The Poetics of Influence,* ed. John Hollander (New Haven: Henry Schwab, 1988), 357.

22. Ibid, 354. That other American Jews share Bloom's feeling is confirmed by David Biale's analysis of contemporary Jewish American political and social ideologies. As he notes, "For some, the success of the American Jewish community is cause for celebration in virtually messianic terms: as opposed to all other Jewish communities, the Jews of America no longer live in exile." David Biale, *Power and Powerlessness in Jewish History* (New York: Schocken Books, 1986), 198.

23. Roth, *The Counterlife,* 323.

24. Ibid., 324.

INDEX